Staff Challenges:

Practical Ideas for Recruiting, Training, and Supervising Early Childhood Employees

Articles from *Exchange* —
The Early Childhood Leaders' Magazine

Exchange Press, Inc.

PO Box 3249 • Redmond, WA 98073-3249 • (800) 221-2864

Staff Challenges:

Practical Ideas for
Recruiting, Training, and Supervising
Early Childhood Employees

This book is a collection of articles from past issues of *Exchange* magazine. The issues in which these articles originally appeared are noted in the Table of Contents.

Every attempt has been made to update information on authors and other contributors to these articles. We apologize for any biograpical information that is not current.

Exchange is a bimonthly management magazine for directors and owners of early childhood programs. For more information about *Exchange* and other *Exchange* publications for directors and teachers, contact:

Exchange Press, Inc.
PO Box 3249
Redmond, WA 98073-3249
(800) 221-2864
info@ChildCareExchange.com

ISBN 0-942702-32-8

Cover Photograph:
Bonnie Neugebauer

Printed in the United States of America

Staff Challenges:

Practical Ideas for Recruiting, Training, and Supervising Early Childhood Employees

— Table of Contents —

Chapter 3 — Orienting and Training Staff

Chapter 4 — Motivating and Supervising Staff

Chapter 5 — Overcoming Challenging Situations

The Paradoxes of Leadership: What We've Learned in 20 Years

by Bonnie and Roger Neugebauer

In the past 20 years, we have had the opportunity to observe hundreds upon hundreds of leaders in action in early childhood programs. In addition, we have had 20 years to develop our leadership on the job as we struggled, sailed, failed, and succeeded in growing Exchange. From all of these experiences, we have learned a few things about the paradoxes of leadership.

Paradox #1
You need to enjoy your work, but you can't avoid the uglies.

Pop psychologists are forever advising "if you're in a job you don't like, get out of it." Easy for them to say. For many people, finding a fun job is simply not an option — there are simply not enough Ben and Jerry's taste tester jobs to go around.

However, for nearly everyone, there are parts of one's job that are enjoyable and parts that are wretched, parts that are stimulating and parts that are boring. In a perfect world, you would be able to delegate the drudge jobs and hold on to the exciting ones.

Unfortunately, this is not a perfect world. While there are many mundane tasks you, the center director, can delegate, there are certain ugly ones that you can't give away, ignore, or avoid. If you listen to the pop psychologists and only attend to the things you enjoy, you're setting your organization up for disaster.

If you don't fire a lousy teacher, her continuing presence will demotivate other teachers and deprive the children of the experiences they deserve. If you hate writing grant proposals, you may miss an opportunity to attract employer support for your center.

Your best bet is to get the ugly jobs out of the way right away. If you procrastinate on the uglies, even when you are working away at jobs you enjoy, this pleasure will be spoiled by the knowledge that the ugly work is still out there. So eat your cauliflower fast, then sit back and enjoy the Cherries Garcia.

Paradox #2
The more staff strive to protect you, the more they hurt you.

Many of us seem to have this need to take care of everyone. We want everyone to be happy, satisfied, productive, supported, connected. It takes a lot of time and energy to Mother Hen the world, but we do it because we need to.

So when the tables turn and staff want to take care of us, it can feel pretty good. It's certainly great to know that others are noticing when we are overburdened, that they see the magnitude of our responsibilities, that they are sensitive to the fact that a piece of information or news might *put us over the top*.

Though done with the best of intentions (of course this could also be done with less positive motivation), this protective behavior will ultimately prove harmful. There will be information missing, holes in the big picture — and this will hinder the effectiveness of your decision making. If you don't know that two staff members are not getting along, that a parent is upset about a staff comment, that the key to the storage unit is missing, that you are running out of peanut butter, things will fall apart when these specifics would inform your decision making.

Staff need to understand that you, as director, need to know everything. Their motivations for protection can be acknowledged and appreciated, while the act of protection can be firmly, continually rejected. Perhaps staff can learn to deliver the bad news with a gentle touch or a chocolate chip cookie (or would we come to fear cookies?).

Paradox #3
When you are most discouraged, you need to be most motivated.

Art Dronen, Roger's high school track coach, had only one piece of advice for all of us would-be heroes — "Ya gotta wanna." We, of course, treated this as trite nonsense. Decades later, Roger now sees that Art was a wise man.

His wisdom is best exemplified in the world of sports where typically athletes' success will in large part be determined by their determination to succeed. We all remember the Swiss female Olympic marathoner who stumbled into the Los Angles Coliseum totally exhausted. She staggered wildly and painfully about the oval, waving off the assistance of her coaches. Finally, she stumbled across the finish line and fell unconscious into the arms of a race official. She had been training for ten years to complete an Olympic marathon, and when her body gave out in total exhaustion 400 yards from the finish line, her sheer determination kept her going until her mission was accomplished.

While center directors are seldom cheered on by a spirited crowd of 100,000, they do frequently demonstrate amazing feats of perseverance.

In fact, it is in the very nature of the director's job to be confronted, on an almost daily basis, with daunting challenges — replacing sick teachers at 6 am, dealing with an accusation of child abuse, juggling cash flow when reserves are depleted, finding a way to get children home from a field trip when the bus breaks down. Confronted with such frustrations, many directors throw in the towel — they either quit or quit caring.

The directors who succeed, and go on to manage the best programs, are those who don't cave in when the going gets tough, those who are determined, against all odds, to maintain a focus on delivering quality services. These directors have a "Ya gotta wanna" attitude that consistently carries them to the finish line.

Paradox #4
To accomplish the most serious results, you need to believe in the value of whimsy.

Never underestimate the value of humor. Why did laughter get the bad rap for indicating lack of seriousness, slacking off? Our staff meetings are great fun. When an outsider overhears the tone of our meetings, he or she will usually comment with something like: "There was so much laughing going on. How do you get anything done?"

It is the laughter that binds us together, that creates an environment and a sense of teamwork that enables people to share their joys and sorrows, as well as their frustrations and needs. People who can laugh at and with each other, trust each other.

Consider the staff meeting when we were in our usual stories with laughter mode and Roger arrived a bit late and announced: "We have a lot of work to get done today, so we'll just

chit chat for a few more minutes and then get down to it." Suddenly, no one had anything to say. We just sat around and ate our lunch and talked through the issues of the day. Laughter was minimized as was the amount of work accomplished.

A playful approach to life issues, whether personal or professional, fosters creative potential, reduces stress, and just makes living a whole lot better.

Paradox #5
The longer you work, the less you are appreciated.

You were hired as director when the center was in the red and struggling to survive. You slashed expenditures to the bone, cracked down on late payments, built up enrollment, and got the center on the right track. Then you steadied the course when a disgruntled former teacher started spreading nasty false rumors; you kept the center going through a flu epidemic; and you even kept things afloat when a glitzy new center opened across the street.

Now you've been on the job 12 years and the center is running as smooth as can be. You naturally assume that, with all your heroic accomplishments in the past, you have a vast store of good will and credibility built up. Then you have to fire a popular teacher for valid reasons, but reasons you can't share with the staff. The teachers revolt and call for your resignation.

What happened to all that credibility? Since you single-handedly saved the center time and time again, why can't they give you the benefit of the doubt now?

The problem is that organizations have short memories. Given normal turnover, many of your teachers weren't even around when you were leaping tall buildings in a single bound. And those who were around, now that times are easier, tend to forget how stressful life was in the past. As a matter of fact, the longer your center sails along smoothly, the more staff may think your job has become a slam dunk, even though it is your brilliant management that is responsible for the good times.

Don't be too harsh on staff for their fickleness. Maybe you are contributing to the problem. Isn't it possible that after all those years of major stress, now you are content to settle into a mode of management that is steadying the course? Just maybe you've become a bit stodgy — reluctant to rock the boat, to try new ventures, to listen to new ideas, to tolerate parents or staff who don't fit a certain profile.

Longevity and credibility don't go hand in hand. Don't ever assume that you have so much good will built up that you can rest on your laurels. The relevant question is: "What have you done for the center and all its players lately that earns their appreciation?"

Paradox #6
Everyone's your friend when things are going well, but your true friends stand by you in the tough times.

When a crisis rears its ugly head, it is your support system that will save you. We have been rescued on many occasions by the concern and response of our friends — and that might very well include you.

Friends are not, in this case, the people who come up with all the platitudes: "This is really good for you." "Every cloud has a silver lining." "Everything works out in the end." People who say such things provide comfort and cry with you (or drive you crazy), but they don't pull you through.

Friends in crisis are the people who really put themselves into your problem, who put their minds and hearts into understanding where you are and what options you have. They are the people who say, "Have you tried . . . ?" "Why wouldn't this work . . . ?" "If other people can do this, why can't you . . . ?" "Here's an idea that might work . . . ."

These are the people who will help you see your way out. They are the people who will expand the boundaries of your thinking, who will challenge you to use the skills you possess (which they might also remind you of). Be sure you have such friends around you. They are honest and blunt — essential and beyond value.

Chapter 1

Recruiting
and
Selecting Staff

Caregivers of Quality: Essential Attributes for Teachers of Young Children

by Sally Cartwright

Building toward a topnotch child care staff is anything but easy. More than love for children, more than training and experience makes a valuable caregiver. Below, named in bold type, are the essential ingredients in caregivers of quality.

Good physical health is a prerequisite for caregivers at work with young children. More difficult to assess is **emotional maturity**. It was clarified by Barbara Biber of Bank Street College of Education when she wrote that a caregiver "needs to be a person so secure within herself that she can function with principles rather than prescriptions, that she can exert authority without requiring submission, that she can work experimentally but not at random, and that she can admit mistakes without feeling humiliated" (Barbara Biber, in *Childhood Education*, March 1948).

One discerns such qualities in a caregiver neither by resumé nor interview, but by observing him at work with children. Watch the caregiver for these qualities, and watch the children as well, for their behavior reflects caregiver competence. Is there cooperative child initiative? Is there a mix of friendly humor and purpose? Most of all, are the children deeply involved in their work and play? Clear, consistent evidence of a caregiver's personal integration and inner sense of security is truly important for his success with children.

A matured and perceptive **kindness** or unconditional love, so important in good caregivers, means both heart and detachment (discussed below) in helping children to help themselves. A good caregiver knows intuitively what child at which moment requires warm and close concern. She is approachable and friendly. She listens well, gives support as needed, and shares in laughter with, not at, the children.

A good caregiver is keenly aware of emotional and physical safety for each child. His care is shown in constructing the environment for active child learning with his discerning choice of equipment, materials, and spacial arrangement within a consistent, predictable program framework. Children need the support of steady, warm approval. A good caregiver may condemn a child's words or action, but not the child himself.

A good caregiver needs courage and integrity. **Courage** means a strong, upbeat will to work through whatever odds for what one most cares about, in this case the children. A courageous caregiver goes to bat for child needs, often working closely with other staff members, parents, and/or community leaders.

Integrity means a well-knit personality along with honesty in all one does. It means what Polonius told his son: "To thine own self be true, and it must follow as the night the day, thou canst not then be false to any man" (Shakespeare).

As caregivers develop **self-awareness**, they improve each quality mentioned as well as self-evaluation. Caregivers may help each other toward self-awareness through constructive criticism with mutual trust and respect. Quiet reflection and professional counseling may help as well. Working with children will sometimes stir emotions from the caregiver's own childhood. A truly fine caregiver will have searched and brought to light salient unconscious factors in herself. She's aware of their influence when at work with children, and steers her own behavior accordingly.

Good caregivers need a **theoretical ground**, a conceptual framework in which to see children. The developmental-interaction point of view put forward by Bank Street College of Education (Betty Boegehold, Harriet Cuffaro, William Hooks, and Gordon Klopf, *Education Before Five*, Bank Street College, 1977; Barbara Biber, Ellen Shapiro, and Elaine Wickens, *Promoting Cognitive Growth from a Developmental-Interaction Point of View*, NAEYC, 1971; and Ellen Shapiro and Barbara Biber, *The Education of Young Children: A Developmental-Interaction Approach*, Teachers College Record, Vol. 74, No. 1, September 1972) is perhaps the most useful foundation and guide for helping youngsters learn at their best. The word *development* suggests a continuing, complex process of growth and learning, while *interaction* occurs internally between the child's emotional, physical, and cognitive growth, and externally between the child and his expanding physical and social environment. The accent is on *integrative* action by the children themselves. Developmental-interaction is clearly aligned with NAEYC's developmentally appropriate practice (Sue Bredekamp and C. Copple, *Developmentally Appropriate Practice in Early Childhood Programs*, NAEYC, 1997).

Research in the last ten years indicates that a caregiver's intellectual understanding of DAP is often sadly unable to implement appropriate practice with the children (Loraine Dunn and Susan Kontos, "What Have We Learned About Developmentally Appropriate Practice?," *Young Children*, July 1997). Hands-on workshops can be somewhat helpful in training caregivers, but protracted, daily participant experience in a early childhood programs environment that supports active child learning, peer cooperation, creativity, and the keen interest shared by the children in their self-impelled work of learning together is by all odds the best training for beginning caregivers.

A good caregiver, daily responsible for child experience, should have, besides the thorough background in developmental psychology mentioned above, the **equivalent of a college graduate's general knowledge**, and effective access to the media, libraries, and the Internet.

Experience with elemental care of our physical environment and with young children's books is also valuable, while a working knowledge of grass-roots democracy will support cooperative learning. It is through cooperative learning experience from age three onward that children gradually come to understand the benefits and responsibilities of democratic community, which, not incidentally, is so important to the health of our country today.

Child care experts know that, aside from their attainment of needed skills, young children do not need proficiency in traditional academic subjects. The salient point is not so much what, but *how*, they learn. And, again, how children learn best is through their own action: asking questions, finding answers, and testing their answers by using them in their work and play, all with adult *guidance*, not didactic instruction. Good caregivers know the value of a child's innate curiosity and deep satisfaction in the experiential learning process. Let no early childhood programs environment dampen a child's interest and joy in learning!

Good caregivers show unfailing **warm respect for and courtesy to children** as a group and to each child as a unique and unrepeatable individual. Helping a child to make constructive, independent choices toward self-disciplined creativity depends very much upon our genuine, full, and caring respect for that child and his way of working, his way of learning. Such respect cannot be accomplished without a very real knowledge of child development, as

well as the personal caregiver qualities of inner security, integrity, and self-awareness.

Allied to respect is a good caregiver's **trust in each child** to find his own way, in a supportive child care environment, toward personal integrity, acceptable behavior, good learning purpose, and ultimately to realize his unique potential. Genuine trust in a child depends on fundamental knowledge of child development, close observation of the individual child, and the caregiver's own inner sense of security mentioned above.

Integrity and respect invite **discretion**. A child's problems should remain confidential. Respect for the privacy of the child and her family is essential for their trust and confidence in the caregiver.

Contrary to strictly linear thinking, which western science and philosophy have championed for three centuries, intuition, a non-reasoning, often quite sudden, insight is finally gaining credence. Einstein said, "Imagination is more important than knowledge," and imagination lives with intuition. For many of us, intuition often sways our thinking simply because it feels right and it works. A well-balanced, mature, and keenly observant caregiver *knows in her bones* how to be with a child.

Professional **detachment** allows respect, trust, and kindness (unconditional love) to come through to the child. On the surface, detachment and love may seem a paradox, but precisely the opposite is true. A caregiver with inner security and mature self-awareness, a caregiver at ease and fulfilled by her own adult development, does not impose her personality needs onto her relations with children.

Detachment in caring allows empathy without projection, without naively attributing her own unconscious negative feelings to the children. Detachment gives the children psychological space. It avoids sarcasm and contempt which are crushing to a child. Detachment helps the caregiver test and use her knowledge of child development with a degree of wisdom.

Don't forget **laughter**. One sign of detachment is often delightful humor, and humor in the classroom is important. It signals enjoyment. It invites friendship. It often opens the way for cooperative learning. While shared humor lights the morning, laughing at a child's expense should be nipped at once. Affectionate laughter is an indispensable quality in good child care.

Finally, the **caregiver is a model.** Whether conscious of it or not, he models feeling, thought, and behavior for the children in his care. An inevitable part of child learning is copying; trying to think, feel, and act like persons consistently near and admired by the child. A beloved provider may demonstrate values which the children cherish all their lives. The personality of a caregiver, her instinctive kindness, her deep integrity, her lively interest in life and learning, will all affect the children. It is a sobering responsibility, an inspiring challenge.

Sally Cartwright, with an MS from Bank Street College of Education, has taught children and teachers across five decades. She has written eight books for children and much material on early childhood learning, especially as experienced in her own experimental school.

Hiring for Professional, Creative Imagination

by Ian Broinowski

The room was vibrant. The children were engrossed; Julie was enchanting as an educator. I was observing Julie and her children making a dinosaur as part of my Ph.D study in a small center in Brisbane, Australia. I was simply entranced by her work. There was a buzz of activity — learning and life going on as I sat enthralled by her almost magical and certainly inspirational involvement with her children and their learning. It was one of those moments we all cherish in our work as teachers — a time we just want to hang onto forever — the smell of glue, the chatter, the creativity, the mess, and the smiles and laughter. All this combined to make something unique, special, and simply beautiful.

But why was it so unusual? The same scene is played out in early childhood programs all over the world every day. Children and their teachers are intertwined as they explore a myriad of activities together. And yet my experience has been that really creative, imaginative, and enchanting programs for young children are the exception.

At another center, I felt a sense of dismay as I observed an all too familiar table of organized collage and paints being prepared by the staff. They were all caring, well-trained educators with a collective wealth of experience, but their work with children was mediocre.

These two cases illustrate my dilemma and has lead me to pursue a constant and perplexing question over the last decade or so. My struggle has been to find out what makes some educators quite simply outstanding in their work. What makes the difference between the two examples above? Why do I inwardly smile when I enter one program with an overwhelming sense of "Oh, wow!" and sigh in the other?

To answer this question I have drawn from the world of art, music, and drama to examine the fundamental notion that perhaps working with young children is in fact more of an art form than a science. This view led me to seriously challenge the almost obsessive reliance on scientific methodology in our study of children.

Just as there are exceptional artists, musicians, writers, and sculptors I wanted to find out what it is about exceptional educators and why they are different. Artists are in some sense enchanted by their work. They, like early childhood educators are delighted, fascinated, and utterly captivated by their work. Artists are charmed by light, colour, shading, and visual expression. An educator, too, is charmed by children, their relationships, and their own incredulity of life.

I also wanted to explore imagination. To imagine is to be human. An artist and an educator both produce ideas; they create mental images of what does not exist, or things they have yet to experience. Imagination is a powerful force in our lives. It has created greatness and great sadness in human history. But all our historical figures in education have possessed powerful imagination.

Eventually my quest lead me to wonder what role professional creativity plays in our work with young children.

Professional creativity and program quality

My examination of these issues did indeed indicate that there is a relationship between an early childhood educator's sense of enchantment, imagination, and creativity and their work with young children. There is a clear correlation between an educator's professional creative imagination and the creativeness of the children in their care and also the quality of their program.

One implication of my study is that staff and students who have a strong sense of professional, creative imagination are likely to provide creative, imaginative, and better quality programs for children. How then can we select staff and students who have a positive professional creative imagination?

Creativity, imagination, and enchantment indicators

There are indicators which allow the ranking of potential staff or students in their professional, creative imagination. These are reflected in a person's disposition and may be discovered through their comments, emotions, and responses in interviews or through the process of creating a personal vision as outlined below. Indicators may also appear in their work, what they do with children, their thinking processes, and their own sense of reflection.

Begin by asking a prospective teacher to create her own personal vision of an ideal children's program:

Create in your mind a wonderful setting where children are able to learn, have fun, cry, explore, and grow. Imagine in your dream that you are moving among the children and other adults. Live your dream. Use all your perceptive skills to discover what makes your vision so

wonderful for children. (Broinowski, 2002, p. 64)

Ask your students or interviewees to explore their ideas using Mind Mapping® techniques. Provide them with plenty of collage materials, paints, glue, natural materials and see what happens.

Allow each person to talk through their ideas and in the process look for their sense of enchantment, imagination, and creativity.

Enchantment

Look for a sense of enchantment in the early childhood educator. To be enchanted is to be delighted or captivated, utterly fascinated, or charmed. This is indicated by an educator's behaviour in such things as:

■ curiosity in ideas, how things work, why things happen, and about the world around them

■ being engrossed in an event or things happening

■ keen sense of interest in many diverse areas.

Imagination

Look for indicators of the educator's or professional's imagination. How imaginative are they in their work with young children? How good are they at producing ideas or creating mental images of what is not present or they have not yet experienced? This may be shown in their behaviour by indicators such as:

■ divergent thinking

■ inventiveness

■ metaphoric thinking

■ abstract thought

■ holistic senses

■ pretending

■ thinking beyond reality.

Creativity

Look for some evidence which shows the educator's ability to bring new ideas into existence and which directly contribute to the quality of their work with young children. This may be shown by the the following indicators (Dalton, 1985, p. 30):

■ Fluency — thinking of many ideas related to a particular topic.

■ Flexibility — thinking about a problem by analysing and finding different approaches or ways of seeing the issue.

■ Originality — including the element of uniqueness.

■ Elaboration — building onto an idea to make it more interesting or complete.

■ Complexity — finding many different and challenging alternatives to a problem. It is also the ability to bring some order out of disorganisation and chaos.

■ Risk taking

■ Imagination — allows people to go beyond the boundaries of reality.

The children's creative imagination

The second way to discover a person's sense of creative imagination is simply allow them the freedom and latitude to devise their own program and to observe them at work. An educator's creative imagination is directly reflected in the creative imagination of the children in their play. More precisely, you are trying to determine whether their program creates a learning experience *which generates potential for children to extend their creative imagination*. Clearly this notion is problematic. Does a lump of playdough on a table by itself have the potential for children to be creative? Children can happily play for hours with just one Lego® person, or with a toy car, or in a pool of mud. It is not the item itself that is creative but rather the creative interaction that the child creates with the object.

There are degrees of potentiality, and, given the right learning environment, children and adults are more likely to be imaginative and creative in their learning. Potentiality for imaginative learning may be seen in child-adult relationships, the environment, and the activity, and may be assessed through observations and discussion.

1. Relationships

Look for the creation of conditions which inspire children. Things like sharing curiosity; expressing a sense of wonder; valuing children's contributions; incorporating and adapting to children's interest and ideas; helping children focus on their own special talents and strengths.

Think about how they show respect for children. Look for their skills in helping children to explore; offering children secure relationships which allow curiosity to flourish and seeing the world through the eyes of children (Duffy, 1998, p. 99). Do they value and emphasise the process as well as the product?

2. Environment

The second significant factor providing the basis for imagination and creativity in young children is the environment. Consider the adult's use of spaces and resources. Look at their design for the environment. Is there time and space for the child to work alone or with groups of children and with adults? Is there a variety of materials for exploration and play? What materials spark exploration and play?

How well does the person ensure that there is enough time and space for the child to work alone as well as with groups of children and with adults? Are children given adequate time in which to develop, explore ideas, and be given encouragement?

3. The Activity

The final factor for imaginative and creative learning potential is the activity itself. Cecil et al. (1985, cited in Duffy, 1998, p. 81) presented an interesting way to support the creative process with four elements: curiosity, exploration, play, and creativity.

Curiosity. What is it? Children are alert, interested, and want to know more. Their attention has been captured.

Exploration. What does it do? Children can be observed actively investigating objects, events, or ideas. They are using all their senses to gather information. Watching others can also be part of their investigation.

Play. What can I do with this? Children initiate a period of total immersion characterised by spontaneity and often without clear final objectives.

Creativity. What can children create or invent? The child discovers uncommon or new approaches to the materials or problem they are investigating, they take risks and make new connections.

Conclusion

There is something intrinsically and innately unique about exceptional early childhood educators. Like brilliant artists they bring something very special to their work. Their presence will add a dimension of rare beauty, wonder, and enchantment in a children's program. By exploring some of the ideas in this article you may be in a better position to find such a person for your program.

I would love to hear from anyone who would like to try out some of these ideas or simply wants to comment. Write to Ian Broinowski: ianb@our.net.au.

References

Anning, A., & Edward, L. (1999). *Promoting Children's Learning from Birth to Five: Developing the New Early Years Professional*. Buchingham: Open University Press.

Buzan, T. (1995). *The Mind Map Book*. London: BBC Books. Mind Map® is a registered trademark of the Buzan organisation, 1990.

Broinowski, I. (2002). *Creative Childcare Practice: Program design in early childhood*. Pearson Education.

Dalton, J. (1985). *Adventures in Thinking*. Melbourne: Thomas Nelson.

Duffy, B. (1998). *Supporting Creativity and Imagination in the Early Years*. First. Supporting Early Learning, Hurst V; Joseph J. Buchingham: Open University Press.

Fielding, R. (1983). "Creativity Revisited: Strategies for Developing Potential." *Journal of Art Education 7*, 2: 51-60.

NCAC, National Childcare Accreditation Council. (2001). *NCAC Source*

Book. ACT: National Childcare Accreditation Council.

Tegano, D. W., Moran, III, J. D., & Sawyers, J. K. (1991). *Creativity in Early Childhood Classrooms*. First. NEA Early Childhood Series. United States: National Education Association.

Mind Map® is a registered trademark of the Buzan Organisation, 1990.

Dr. Ian Broinowski, Ph.D, Med, BA (Soc Wk), BEc, Dip Teach, is currently an advanced skills teacher in children's services at the Institute of TAFE Tasmania in Hobart, Australia. Ian has a background in Economics, Social Work, and Education. He has taught a wide range of subjects in aged care, disability services, children's services, community, and youth work. He worked for a period as a house parent in Bristol, England and Northern Ireland. He has also held positions as a child welfare officer in Tasmania and NSW. Ian's publications include Child Care Social Policy and Economics, (1994) Creative Childcare Practice: Program design in early childhood, (2002) and recently Managing Children's Services 2004. He has spent the last five years studying for his Ph.D at the University of South Australia in which he examined the relationship between enchantment, imagination, and creativity and the quality of the work of the early childhood educator. Ian was awarded the Jean Denton National Scholarship in 2001.

Assessing Your Center to Create a Diverse Staff

by Katherine S. Kolozak

Monday morning in the United States marks the beginning of a traditional work week when a large majority of families place their children in early childhood programs. Zoom into your typical preschool classroom consisting of 12 children and two staff members. Diversity is represented in the faces and experiences of the children. Johnny comes from your typical nuclear family, Nina is blind in one eye, both Carmen and Kasia are first generation Americans whose parents speak English as a second language, Ally is adopted, Doug's family consists of two fathers, Lucy's parents are divorced, Jason is Jewish, Arun is Muslim, Riley comes from a single family home, Jasmine is African-American and Susie's family receives a third-party subsidy to attend the center. Can the preschool staff weave together the diversity of the children to create a meaningful environment for all children present?

This preschool room is a microcosm of the diversity we all encounter daily. In order for our children to succeed in a diverse society, it is necessary to educate the world's teachers to embrace, value, and create multi-culturally friendly class-rooms. What is valuing diversity? Simply defined, valuing diversity is embracing and incorporating the unique experiences, culture, and life practices of others to create a more cohesive view of the world. Looking at the world with open eyes and an open mind, we allow people to express their views and talents in ways that otherwise might not be explored. Having a staff who can incorporate the unique experiences of all children in the program helps to contribute to a well-rounded society that embraces and values diversity.

Equally important, today's increasingly competitive business environment necessitates that we continually search for ways to attract families and children to our center. By embracing the diversity in our centers, we are also contributing to creating a more inclusive center that better meets the needs of the communities we serve.

Now that we recognize the importance of valuing diversity in the child care/enrichment environment, we must evaluate our current programs/staff to assess their strengths and weaknesses. How do directors go about assessing their center and staff? Further, how can directors help to contribute to creating a more diversified staff? Throughout the remainder of this article, we will explore the steps necessary to assess your center and staff. Then we will further examine what resources are available to help create a diversified staff.

Step One: Education

What do you know about diversity? In order to accurately assess your current program, you must first educate yourself. This self-study will help you define your idea of diversity. Most importantly, you will begin to identify your own biases surrounding diversity. Recognizing your own biases gives you the opportunity to evaluate your hiring practices. Making hiring decisions based solely on the quality of the candidate and the needs of the center assists in creating a more diversified staff.

Step Two:
Your community, parents, and children

Begin by looking at the community that surrounds your center. This will give you a good idea of the population that you serve. Reflect the spirit of your community in your center to bring greater enrollment. Parents' needs will be met in the diverse environment you create. Network with local early care and education providers; this will serve as a great way to share knowledge. Use your licensor as a resource; licensors often know of free training resources in the community they manage. Contact local merchants, restaurants, and places of worship, etc. Visit local community centers to learn of upcoming events. Visit local elementary schools to see if the student population mirrors your center. Join the PTA to keep abreast of the school population and local issues. The PTA can also prove a great resource to parents and staff through community events the organization sponsors. Examining your community will also give you a snapshot of your hiring pool. Your recruitment process will also become enriched as you utilize other avenues to find quality staff.

Who are the parents in the center? Learning about the parents you serve will help you to better understand and teach their children. You might want to consider hosting a parents' night or conducting an optional survey; however, these steps might not meet your parents' needs. Your partnerships with the local early care and education providers, PTA, and licensor might yield more information about your parents. Taking the time to examine your parents' wants and needs for their children's education provides you the opportunity to focus your staff's efforts. Also, this allows you to recognize shortcomings in your current staff, which gives you greater recruitment focus.

Most important, what does your student population look like? In the typical preschool room previously described, there were many examples of diversity. Today, more than ever, the classrooms in our centers are filled with children from many walks of life. Assessing the children in your center should be coupled with parent assessment. Begin by carefully reviewing your enrollment packets. This will assist in shedding some light on your center's diversity. Follow up with parents regarding any questions you might have. Also, include your teachers in the assessment of the children. Since the teachers spend a majority of their day with the children, they will be able to provide further insight. Exploring the diversified needs of the children in your programs should help guide your training and hiring decisions.

Step Three:
Your staff

Complete a thorough assessment of your staff to identify their strengths and weaknesses with regard to implementing diversity in their programs. Your staff serves as the catalyst to celebrate the differences each child offers. It is also important that your staff incorporates the diversity that is *not* represented in the center. As our society grows more and more diverse, it's important to teach children to respect and value what is different. Can your staff meet the needs of the community, parents, and children? If not, does your current staff need further training to incorporate diversity into their programs? Does your staff reflect your community's diversity? This brings us to an examination of your recruitment process.

Step Four:
What next??

Taking the time to educate yourself, assess your community, and learn

about parents, children, and staff will provide you with an overwhelming amount of information. Begin assimilating the information by identifying what diversity consists of in your center. At the very least, does your staff mirror the diversity of your parents and children? Does the staff incorporate and acknowledge the diversity represented in their classrooms?

Next, identify your center's strengths and weaknesses that contribute to creating diverse programs. Of the strengths identified, ask yourself if they meet the needs of your children and parents. This is a good place to begin to build the basics of a diversified program, as it will meet the immediate needs of your children and parents. Little by little, you can then begin to incorporate other examples that contribute to a diverse program.

Most importantly, can your staff accomplish the goals you have set for your center? In Step Three, you conducted a thorough self-assessment of your staff and identified how each staff member contributed to a diverse curriculum for the program. You probably also identified staff who were not contributing to building a diversified program. As you move forward into the next section, focus your efforts on resources to create and maintain a diverse staff.

Resources for creating a diverse staff focused on diversity

One of the most important steps in creating a staff attuned to diversity is education. It is not that teachers are unwilling to implement diversity in their programs. They often do not know where to start. Many colleges offer classes on multicultural curriculum. Inquire at the local colleges and community colleges to learn more about the programs these schools offer. Research any grants currently available to support teacher education. Receiving a source of funding to lead your diversity initiative will showcase your dedication to creating an inclusive program.

There are several routes toward creating a diverse staff. Research the many affiliations and memberships you can join that contribute to creating and maintaining a more diversified staff. Of course, you should join your local NAEYC and NSACA affiliate; NAEYC and NSACA are committed to providing education and resources to teachers. NAEYC and NSACA standards also reflect the commitment to multicultural classrooms/programs. Aside from educational affiliates, explore joining your local Chamber of Commerce and Better Business Bureau. These organizations tend to be up to date on your community's trends and demographics. They also serve as a great way to network with other businesses in the service industry.

Broadening your teacher recruitment resources will lead to a more diversified staff. Examine the current methods you utilize to recruit new teachers; what could you do differently? Recruiting at local colleges and researching your community's minority and diversity organizations could enhance your staff's diversity.

You might already recruit at local colleges, but are you maximizing the possibilities? Begin your recruitment visit with a trip to student services; find out what majors are offered and what organizations/clubs are active. Often you can find an excellent teacher outside of the traditional early childhood or elementary education department. Consider looking at the psychology, sociology, women studies, ethnic studies departments, etc. Typically these departments have a strong focus on children. Also, visit the different language departments. This is a great place to find a teacher who speaks a second language. You might also want to stop by the drama/music department. Sourcing a teacher who can teach the children other creative forms of expression is invaluable.

Now, you can begin learning more about the organizations/clubs on campus, many of which reflect diversity. Typically, organizations that reflect diverse minority groups are affiliated with each department, such as organizations that support persons with disabilities, etc. The recruitment options at local colleges are endless once you start examining the possibilities.

Finally, a few other ideas. Talk to your staff and parents; find out if they are members of any community organization. Your phone book is an excellent resource as well. It will provide contact information for some of the larger organizations. The Internet can also provide community information. Take the time to conduct an Internet search using key words. You can use an Internet search engine to search for different organizations that match your center's needs. For example, you could search for Hispanic organizations in the city and state in which you live.

When we began, our typical preschool room was enriched by the wealth of its diversity. However, it is possible that the staff was not as diverse as the children they serve. It is also possible that the staff was not doing enough to reflect and embrace the diversity of the children they serve. Assessing your center and staff involves self-education and an assessment of your community, children, parents, and staff.

Once you have completed your assessment, implement changes with the resources available to you in your community. Even *baby steps* will move you in the right direction as you seek to create a diverse staff that incorporates a multicultural curriculum and recognizes and celebrates the diverse communities in which we live and serve.

Katherine Kolozak, PHR, is a Regional Human Resource Manager at Knowledge Learning Corporation. She is a graduate of the University of Washington. Katherine is a member of the Society of Human Resource Management from which she received her PHR certification. She has been with Knowledge Learning Corporation for over six years supporting the Human Resource Department.

Out of Site But Not Out of Mind: The Harmful Absence of Men

by Bruce Cunningham and Bernie Dorsey

Over the years we have spoken on the topic of male involvement at many conferences, workshops, and staff meetings. We are often asked a variety of questions on how to involve fathers and other men in the lives of children. Recently, we were asked a particularly intriguing question by the director of an early care and education center.

In this situation, a single father enrolled his child in the director's early childhood center. When the father was asked about the child's mother he replied that the mother was "not in the picture." This alone is not so unusual because approximately 20% of single parents are fathers according to U.S. Census Bureau statistics. What was unusual was the staffing at the early childhood center. The classroom into which the child entered had a man as the teacher and another man as the teacher assistant.

The director describing this situation felt the quality of care in the classroom was very good and did not doubt that the child would be well cared for. Yet the questions asked of us were, "Doesn't this child need to be around women? Won't the child be deprived if raised only around men? Won't the child only learn about women from distorted images in the media? And what if the father is saying uncomplimentary things about the mother — won't that damage this child's view of women now and later in life?"

The person asking these questions was genuinely concerned, and the questions were remarkable. Remarkable not for what they asked, but for what they didn't ask about the more common absence of men in the lives of children. It is much more common in early childhood programs that a single mother enrolls a child. It is more common that no one inquires about the presence of a father or other man in that child's life. It is more common that the child's teachers and caregivers will all be women. The number of men teaching in pre-kindergarten programs is estimated by a recent survey of National Association for the Education of Young Children (NAEYC) to be about 3%. The number of men teaching in elementary grades is estimated by the National Education Association for Elementary Teachers to be 13%, with most of these found in the fifth and sixth grades.

Furthermore, it is more common that the child will learn a good deal of what they know about men from television and other media sources. A 1999 study by the National Fatherhood Initiative found that television programs seldom featured fathers and when they did, fathers were likely to be portrayed as a competent man yet uninvolved father or an involved father yet an incompetent man. Another 1999 study, "Boys to Men: Media Messages About Masculinity" by the advocacy group Children Now, found that television programs most often portrayed men as violent and angry and rarely showed men in nurturing or home life situations.

The director who asked the questions during the training was correct in that children are strongly influenced by the experiences they have over time. She was right that children need men and women in their lives. And she was reassured to hear that the child in this situation will have positive personal experiences with women — if not in the early childood center then certainly later on in school.

Unfortunately, many children do not have men as positive role models while growing up. Many children do not get the benefits in intellectual development and social competence that an involved man contributes. According to a 1999 Child Trends Research Brief, these contributions come through parenting and play styles of fathers that are unique from those of mothers. It is not reassuring that children are being harmed by this absence of men.

To address this more common situation, early care and education centers can take the following actions:

■ Shift your view from fathers (which tends to connote the biological father only) to fathering (men who nurture children including biological fathers). The biological father plays a critical role in our culture, in the lives of children, and in the importance of knowing about the genetic influences in your own family health history. Yet many men can fulfill the nurturing role of fathering by being that positive man in the life of a child.

■ Help each family identify a man for each child at the time of enrollment. This can be the biological father, a step-father, a grandfather, uncle, or family friend. Any man who has a positive relationship with a child can build on that relationship to benefit the child.

■ Inform families of your center philosophy that children already have both men and women who are already involved in their lives. Identify, reach out, and support these adults in their involvement with their child. Make your expectations clear that both parents —

or a man and a woman — are expected to participate in center activities such as parent conferences.

■ Send program information to the men. A man can be involved with a child only when he knows what is going on in the life of that child. Early childhood programs can communicate much through newsletters, by talking with men, and by personally inviting men to attend parent and family events.

■ Recruit men into the program as staff and regular volunteers. Many men, from high school students to senior citizens, enjoy spending time with young children and will do so if asked and welcomed.

■ Inform men about special programs for new dads even if they are already a father. A growing number of these programs, such as Boot Camp for New Dads and Conscious Fathering reach men through childbirth classes. These programs offer information tailored to men at a highly teachable moment, even if the child to be born is not their first.

While men are often out of early childhood sites, they are seldom out of the minds of children. These actions can help child care programs connect more children with men. As a result, we will have strong programs for families and better lives for children.

Resources to support directors, staff, and families

■ Boot Camp for New Dads
www.newdads.com

■ Child Trends
www.childtrends.org

■ Children Now
www.childrennow.org

■ Conscious Fathering Programs
www.helpfordads.com

■ National Fatherhood Initiative
www.fatherhood.org

■ National Association for the Education of Young Children
www.naeyc.org
(printed brochures *Involving Men in the Lives of Children*, order #593 and *Careers for Men in Early Childhood Education*, order #594)

Bruce Cunningham has worked in early childhood settings as an assistant, a teacher, a director, and an educator. He is currently an education coordinator with the Early Childhood Education and Assistance Program (ECEAP) through the Puget Sound Educational Service District in Seattle, Washington.

Bernie Dorsey is the founder of Conscious Fathering Programs. His "Skills for New Dads" hospital based program has graduated over 3,000 men in the Puget Sound area and in addition, over 11,000 of Bernie's Guide for Expectant Fathers have been distributed statewide. Bernie is also one of the recipients of the Governor's 2002 Award for Advocacy of Child Abuse Prevention. As a member of the Leadership Group for the Washington State Fathering Coalition, Bernie continues to work at encouraging parentally balanced programs for families.

Guidelines for Effective Staff Selection

by Carl C. Staley, Jr., Edna Runnels Ranck, Joe Perreault, and Roger Neugebauer

All I have to do is talk to a person for five minutes and I know whether she will be a good teacher or not.

Everyone's heard at least one director make a boast like this. To this director, staff selection is no mystery. More often than not, however, this person is exhibiting self-deception more than self-confidence.

Selecting the right person to work with young children in a early childhood setting has never been an easy task. How can you be sure which candidate will be able to nurture children, challenge children to grow, establish rapport with parents, and work well with the other teachers; and who will be able to do all this for low pay in a church basement 35 hours a week for 50 weeks a year? Certainly not in a five minute conversation.

And the job just got tougher. On the one hand, sex abuse scandals have chased many good candidates out of the field of early childhood, and have also made directors, parents, and public officials highly conscious of the need to screen out potential abusers from working with children. On the other hand, looming staffing shortages are shrinking the pool of teaching candidates. So now directors are faced not with selecting the best candidate from a long list of highly qualified applicants but, more often than not, with finding a low-risk, acceptable choice from a handful of marginally qualified applicants.

To be effective under all these restraints, a selection process needs to be well planned and carefully executed. The following are some guidelines on how to accomplish this. At the close of the article are some additional resources to pursue for more detailed assistance in upgrading your selection process.

Planning for success

Time invested in planning the selection process will yield valuable returns in the smooth operation of your program. The following three areas need particular attention before you screen your first resumé.

• **Clarify your objectives**

Obviously the prime objective of the selection process is to secure the best available individual for a position. However, there are two additional not-so-obvious objectives that people involved in the hiring process must appreciate:

1. To sell the organization to the candidates. What good does it do to select just the right candidate only to have her turn down the job because she gained a negative impression of your organization during the selection process? While you are checking out the candidates, they are checking out your organization as well. It is in the best interests of both parties to make a favorable impression. Even candidates who are turned down should leave feeling that they were treated fairly and respectfully. Sore losers can do much to damage your reputation in the community.

2. To initiate the contractual process. Job advertisements and job interviews should be treated as the first steps in the process of negotiating a contract. A new employee's commitment to the center may be seriously undermined if the center reneges on promises made or expectations aroused during the selection process.

• **Prioritize qualifications**

Whenever a position becomes vacant, it is a good opportunity to take a close look at what qualifications are really needed for adequate performance. It may be helpful to sort out those qualifications which are *required* (by licensing, funding, or operating agencies), *essential* (to implement the goals and philosophy of your center), and *desirable* (to perform in an exceptional fashion). During the selection process, your prime attention should be devoted to assessing candidates in terms of the *essential* qualifications.

To keep your attention from being diffused in too many directions, you should try to narrow your list down to four or five qualifications. If your list is too long, try putting them in priority order in terms of the impact they have on job performance. Then, in the selection process, focus on the four or five that make the biggest impact.

Once you have identified the qualifications list, you should put yourself in the role of a detective. Your job in the selection process is to methodically ferret out pieces of evidence as to whether the candidates do or don't meet these qualifications. Adopting such an attitude can prevent you from being misled by general impressions or irrelevant factors.

• **Select your evaluation tools**

In preparing to screen job candidates, you have a number of tools at your disposal. None of these tools can provide you with all the information you need to make a decision. Therefore, it is best to evaluate candidates with a combination of tools. At a minimum, you will want to screen

written applications, conduct interviews, and check references.

There are other steps you may want to consider as well. For example, most centers try to observe candidates working with children. Since the way teachers describe their teaching behavior in an interview often bears little relation to how they perform in real life, such observations can provide invaluable feedback. Some centers have gained insights into candidates' teaching styles by having them build whatever they want with blocks. Other centers have learned about candidates' teaching philosophies by having them design on paper their ideal classroom.

Many states now require centers to pursue criminal records checks on prospective employees in order to prevent sex offenders from being employed in centers. However, the center certainly should never use criminal records checks in lieu of interviews and reference checks.

Screening applications

The review of written submissions provides an efficient means of assessing candidates' work experience and academic preparation but not much beyond that. As such, they should be used primarily to screen out candidates who do not meet the minimum job requirements.

This preliminary screening is most reliable if it can be based on information provided on application forms developed by the center. Resumés tend to be less useful sources; the way candidates present their qualifications can exclude or cover up information which reflects poorly on them. A center-designed application forces candidates to present all needed information in a uniform, understandable format.

In reviewing written submissions, look for long gaps between jobs,

lengthy descriptions of educational experiences, an overabundance of personal trivia (resumés puffed up with hobbies, scouting awards, etc.), long lists of short-term jobs, employment and training situations which run concurrently, long stretches of employment outside one's field of specialization, and evidence that one may have been fired. Findings such as these should be viewed as red flags to be investigated, not necessarily as grounds for rejection. A teacher may have been fired from a job, for example, but maybe because her boss was unstable and not because of her inadequacies.

Conducting interviews

The interview can be very helpful in revealing the personality of candidates, their communication skills, and their knowledge of early childhood education. However, it is the most complex selection tool, and its advantage can be lost if it is not carefully planned and executed.

• **Logistics**. Be sure to allow sufficient time to interview candidates in depth at a relaxed pace. Set aside at least 45 minutes for each interview and schedule a 15 minute break between each interview. Try not to schedule more than three interviews consecutively or mental fatigue may set in.

Don't create a Spanish Inquisition setting. A candidate walking into a room with a panel of 12 interviewers can't help but become anxious. The more people a candidate is interviewed by, the harder it will be for him to relax and give a fair accounting of himself. Restricting the number of interviewers may fail to satisfy all constituencies within the organization, and it may mean that certain points of view are not adequately represented. But having too many interviewers will inhibit an open exchange. Ideally, the director and one other person should conduct the interview. One person can lead the conversation and the second can observe for body language and tone of voice.

Plan ahead for recording information. By the end of an interview, interviewers generally have already forgotten 50% of what was said. By the next day, 85% of what was said has been lost in space (Nichols). The best method for recording information is tape recording. Candidates may find this disconcerting initially; but after a few minutes, they will forget the recorder is on. The next best method is to take notes onto a specific format with spaces set aside for each qualification. In either case, interviewers should also write down their reactions immediately after the interview.

• *Questioning.* Your initial objective in the interview should be to put the candidate at ease. You can do this by finding some point of common interest on the application and commenting on it: "I see you grew up in the Midwest just like I did; do you ever think about moving back?" Then lead into the interview with some specific, easy-to-answer questions.

The pattern of questioning that has been found to be most effective for the substantive portion of the interview is to spend some time pursuing each essential qualification. Lead off with a prepared introductory question or two, and then follow up by asking specific spontaneous questions which seek clarification of issues raised in the candidate's response. Liberal use of the word *why* can move a candidate away from her cautious, programmed replies.

If, for example, the candidate states that she loves to work with kids, follow up with "Why do you find this so rewarding?" or "What activities do you most like to do with children?"

It is usually a mistake to ask trick questions or to purposely put the can-

didate under stress with threatening or overly personal questions. This creates an atmosphere of mistrust and tension. Much more can be learned by straightforward, respectful questioning.

Don't do all the talking. The more you talk, the less you learn about the candidate. Keep the candidate talking by responding with phrases such as "I understand," "I see," or "That's very interesting," which encourage her to continue but don't give any clues as to whether you are reacting positively or negatively to what she is saying. Encourage honesty and openness by praising her for answering questions fully and frankly.

Close the interview by describing the organization and the position, and by expressing a willingness to answer questions about the position. Explain the process that will follow, and let the candidate know when and how he will be notified of the final decision.

Checking references

Information obtained from checking references may be the only effective way to evaluate many qualifications, such as dependability, flexibility, initiative, and communication with parents. Checking references can also serve to verify information gathered in other portions of the process.

On your center's application form, or when you call to set up interviews, you should alert candidates to the fact that you intend to contact references to verify their job qualifications. Be wary of those candidates who balk at supplying any references or who supply only the names of personal (non-employer) references, as they may well have something to hide.

• **Selecting references**

You should not limit yourself to contacting references supplied by the candidate. As a matter of practice, you should always contact at least one reference not supplied by the candidate. In today's nervous climate, you may do well to routinely contact a candidate's last three employers. Contact first the head of each organization, and at the close of the interview ask for the name of someone else in that organization who may have worked directly with the candidate. Then contact this employee for an additional point of view.

Sometimes a candidate will ask that you not contact his current employer because he doesn't want his boss to know he is job hunting. This may be a legitimate request or it may be a ruse for avoiding a negative reference. You should honor this request with the proviso that if the job is offered it will be contingent upon the receipt of a favorable reference from the current employer.

The best reference of all is someone you know. This person is likely to know the type of person you are looking for and is more likely than a person who doesn't know you to give a candid appraisal. For that reason, when you are seriously considering employing someone, you should put your antenna up in the community to see if anyone on your staff or any of your parents knows this person and can provide a reference.

Another approach is to get to know officials at the local or state level who are responsible for receiving child care related complaints. Routinely run the names of persons you are about to hire past these officials to see if they have been identified in any complaints.

• Soliciting information

Securing candid information from references is no easy matter. Especially in today's suit-happy society, employers are not eager to offer less

than favorable references. As Robert Half laments, "A bad reference is as hard to find as a good employee."

As a general rule, the more personal your means of contact, the more candid views you are likely to receive. Letters of recommendation that candidates attach to their resumés are not likely to be of any value whatsoever. Reference letters supplied at your request will only be slightly more useful. People are highly resistant to putting any but the most guarded, neutral statements in writing. For best results, you should contact references over the telephone. Better yet, for critical positions, it may even be worthwhile to interview references in person.

• Probing for information

There are a number of techniques you can employ to make references more forthcoming. To begin with, when you call, you might find it less intimidating to say you are seeking verifications rather than references. Lead off with factual questions such as dates of employment, position title, and responsibilities, and then gradually move on to more subjective questions.

Ask the employer being interviewed if she would hire the candidate again. If she answers no, or if there is a noticeable hesitation in her reply, probe the response in more depth. Use silence to get the reference talking. After she has given a cursory response to one of your questions, don't respond. Give her an opportunity to get nervous about the silence. She just may attempt to fill it by elaborating upon her response.

If the interviewee is still being reticent, you may find it helpful to note that with all the attention on incidents of abuse in centers, you really need help in carefully screening candidates who will be working with

children. Describe the candidate's potential position, as well as center and state policies on child discipline and sexual abuse. Ask if the candidate, in her view, would have any difficulty complying with these procedures.

Be wary of references that are overwhelmingly positive or negative, as there may be some ulterior motive in operation. Be wary as well of major discrepancies between references' and candidates' reports. In both cases, be sure to track down at least a second or third opinion.

Making the decision

This is the stage where the process most often goes awry. All too often center representatives will knock themselves out reading resumés, conducting interviews, and checking references. Then, when they get to the point of making a decision, they make a snap judgment based on *gut feelings* alone, a decision which as often as not they live to regret.

The most common cause for errors at the decision point is the *halo effect* — letting one outstanding characteristic (positive or negative) of a candidate shape the opinion about her overall suitability. For example, in an interview one of the candidates may display a tremendous amount of personal charm and vitality which deeply impresses the interviewer. This impression may cause him to overlook the fact that the candidate had a reputation for absenteeism and irresponsibility at her previous two jobs.

To arrive at a sound decision, it is helpful to follow through on the detective approach. For each candidate, consider what pieces of evidence were uncovered in terms of each qualification. When you look at the pattern of evidence, how many of the qualifications did each candidate display? The decision comes down then to considering the weight of the evidence as opposed to subjective impressions.

Don't rush this stage of the process. You should even be willing to go back and call a candidate or two for a second interview if you have some nagging doubts. An hour or two saved at this point may cost you days later on if the candidate you select doesn't work out and you have to start all over again.

Another safeguard worthy of consideration is placing new employees on probationary status. This puts them on notice that you will be carefully monitoring their performance at the outset to make sure it conforms with expectations raised during the selection process. When you have made your decision, notify the candidate you have selected by telephone, and follow up with a letter outlining the title of the position, rate of pay, starting date, benefits, and length of the probationary period. If the candidate accepts this offer, notify all other candidates of this decision, including those who were eliminated early in the process.

References and resources

Half, R. (1985). *Robert Half On Hiring*. New York: Crown Publishers, Inc.

Ingber, D. (September 1984). "Omigod, I've Hired a Turkey!" *Success*.

Nichols, R. (September-October, 1957). "Listening to People." *Harvard Business Review*.

"Preventing Sexual Abuse in Day Care Programs." Office of Inspector General, United States Department of Health and Human Services, Region X, January 1985.

Viscott, D., MD (1985). *Taking Care of Business*. New York: William Morrow and Company.

An Experiential Approach to Staff Selection

by Merle W. Leak

When is the last time you played with blocks? If you had been applying for a position in the early childhood agency I directed you would have been able to relive this bit of childhood as part of the interview process. You also would have had the opportunity to explore cartoons, design a room, write about your childhood, and tell me what you think of Sesame Street. All these activities are parts of an experiential staff selection process I designed and utilized with the Bucks County Coordinated Child Care Council in Southampton, Pennsylvania.

This selection process grew out of some real discouragement with the normal selection techniques. So often in early care and education we come to selection decisions which turn out not to be good ones. I believe that in the early childhood setting it is very important to achieve a real match between the person selected and the setting in which they will work. If a very controlling, structured person is elected to teach in a center with an open and creative philosophy, everybody is going to be unhappy — the director, the other teachers, and the new teacher. Unfortunately, with the selection techniques normally used in early childhood, we often can't learn enough to make such a match. We are not able to discover what the candidates are really like as persons.

Therefore, I set out to develop a selection process that gave people an opportunity to say something to me about themselves through other means than verbal responses to questions. I wanted a process that would show me something not only about what the candidates knew, but also something about them as persons — what they thought about children, the world, and themselves.

The process that resulted was used with great success by the Bucks County Coordinated Child Care Council. The process was used by myself and other agency personnel in screening over 500 candidates when we were setting up eight new centers and filling later vacancies in these centers. I will describe the process we used, but I don't necessarily recommend that other centers use it exactly as is. Rather, it should be viewed as an example of the types of experiential techniques that can be employed by centers to get to know candidates better in order to achieve a successful match.

The selection process

The selection process I developed had seven components. These components were used as the initial screening process for directors, educational supervisors, head teachers, and early childhood workers. For a typical position there were usually 50 to 60 applications. Of these we selected about 10 to 20 to screen with the seven step process in order to recommend two or three candidates. The candidates who survived this initial screening were then interviewed by a parent board and/or a center director, and sometimes observed in the classroom, before a final decision was made.

Our hiring process was a very serious one and a very long one. Since all of us in the agency were convinced that the adults working with the children are the key to the success of a child care program, we were willing to invest the number of hours needed to find the right match. The seven step screening process described usually required 1½ to 2 hours for each position. Some screenings lasted as long as 4 to 5 hours as we never put an outer limit on the time allotted to candidates.

Resumé Reviews. The first step in the screening process was a review of the candidates' education and experience as described in their resumes in terms of the specific job requirements. We tended to give the benefit of doubt in reviewing resumes to things that went beyond normal degrees and things like that. We had a feeling that there probably would be some good people who would be lost if we only looked for degrees in early childhood education. As a result, we probably accepted an unusually large number of candidates for extensive screening — as many as 10 to 20 per position. These candidates were invited for the remainder of the screening which always took place in a center that had a complete set of Community Playthings' nursery school blocks.

Personal Interviews. When a candidate arrived at the center he or she was interviewed by one staff person for about 20 to 30 minutes. At the outset, the interviewer talked a little bit about the job and explained the process that was to follow. Then each candidate was asked seven questions. We kept the format and the questions the same for each candidate in order to have comparable responses. The seven questions looked at three things: interest in and knowledge about child development, specific relevant skills, and who the candidates were as individuals. The questions were:

- What does fantasy have to do with childhood?

- What are the three most significant books that you have read in the past twelve months?

- What does open education mean to you?

- What is your favorite story or picture book for children?

- What does the phrase "you cannot teach anyone anything" mean to you?

- What do you think of Sesame Street?

- At what age do children begin to form peer relationships?

Block Building. After the interview, the candidates were brought into the room with the complete set of blocks. They were instructed that what they were to do was to build whatever they wanted to and to take as much time as they needed. When they were finished, a picture was taken of their final product. They were told they could share their thoughts on what they had constructed or they could say nothing and that was fine. After the first time we also learned to ask the candidate to put away the blocks — otherwise the person doing the interviewing would spend the rest of his life putting away blocks.

Some candidates completed their structures in 15 to 20 minutes, whereas others plugged away for well over an hour. I particularly remember one woman who worked on something for nearly an hour, and when she added the last block to the top the entire structure collapsed. So she turned around and built an entirely different structure for 45 minutes more.

Cartoon Exploration. The balance of the process was in writing. The candidates were ushered to a quiet room, given instructions for the remaining four parts and invited to take as much time as they required. The first written portion provided candidates an opportunity to respond to five cartoons. These cartoons zeroed in on early childhood settings and were selected in order to illicit candidates' feelings about working with young children in a group setting and what their priorities were. For example, one cartoon depicts a little girl holding a sloppy paint brush, covered from head to toe with paint, standing in the midst of paint containers and paint slopped all over the floor, exclaiming to an adult — "Art is my favorite interest center!" Responses varied from suggestions on controlling children's access and use of art materials in order to avoid messes to opinions that children's exploration of various art medium should not be inhibited in any way.

Sentence Completion. Candidates were given the opening phrase of fifteen sentences and asked to complete them in their own terms. The fifteen were traditional sentence completions such as:

"A child feels unhappy when . . . "

"Teachers need . . . "

"Children are wonderful, but . . . "

Autobiographical Questions. In order to get a broader picture of what the candidates were like, we asked them to respond to the following four autobiographical questions:

- What were you like as a child?

- Give a picture of your family life as a child?

- What were the meaningful relationships of your childhood?

- What kind of children interest you?

Evaluating the results

None of the questions or tasks had right and wrong responses. However, in each instance there were certain types of responses we were looking for. Before administering the test we went through and identified the range of responses we would look for given our philosophy and attitudes. Then in evaluating the candidates' responses we liked for those that were closest to our responses. In this way we were able, in almost every hiring, to achieve a successful match between the person hired and the center they worked in.

In general, we were looking for people who were open, creative, caring, growing individuals. Therefore, we looked for people who demonstrated these characteristics in their responses. In the "art is my favorite interest area" cartoon, for example, we tended to prefer those who laid stress on encouraging children's exploration rather than on those whose prime concern was with keeping the mess under control.

As another example let's consider interview question #6 — "What do you think of Sesame Street?" From those candidates who had seen Sesame Street we tended to get three types of responses. There were many who thought Sesame Street was marvelous — the most wonderful thing that had ever happened to children in the United States. Then there were some who said it was absolutely terrible because no child should ever be encouraged to sit in front of a TV. We tended to like and look for those who gave a third, more thoughtful response. They took the time to point out some of the positive aspects of Sesame Street as well as some of the negative aspects.

The block building results were a most instructive part of our evaluation process. First as you can see varying degrees of openness and creativity in the block building of children, the same can be seen in that of adults. I believe that the block building of adults and children has very similar stages and patterns. Its openness or closeness and the nature of its creativity reflects an enormous amount about the person — who they are, their possible ways of working with young children, and their approach to something new. Candidates' structures varied

between two extremes. At the one extreme were tiny square buildings with roofs and no windows. These certainly conveyed a very closed, tight feeling without any real expression. At the other extreme were the structures which recreated whole cities or, in one instance, a beautiful flower garden. These very open creative structures were clearly what we were looking for.

In the overall evaluation of a candidate's responses, we never zeroed in on any one thing. We always looked at the total package. The candidate's responses in all seven components were considered together to form a more complete picture. What we generally found, however, is when the match was there in one or two cartoons, it was also there in the interviews and the block building. In other words, there turned out to be a high degree of consistency in what was revealed by these various techniques.

Candidates' reactions and responses

In the five and one-half years I used this process, I never had anyone who was reluctant to do it. Some reacted to the block building portion with amazement, but then settled down and dug right into it. Most candidates actually seemed to enjoy and, in many cases, appreciate the process. At the end one candidate said it was one of the most fascinating interviews she had ever had, that it was the first time a selection process was really being taken seriously, and the first time she felt she had a chance to show who she really was. Similar sentiments were frequently expressed by candidates.

Even though candidates willingly and often eagerly took part in the process, I was continually amazed at the range of performance levels. In the interview portion, for example, I was amazed at how few people

could ever name an appropriate children's story book. When it came to room design, extremely few candidates were able to recreate what many of us would feel were appropriate early childhood settings with interest areas, various ways of blocking off the room, etc. Most designed what looked like a typical first grade room with desks and chairs in rows and a teachers desk and an American flag up front. Those who employed more open designs often tended to build all the activity areas around the four walls and leave a great vacant space in the middle. What is even more amazing is that the candidates often created these inadequate designs while seated in the midst of a well-designed early childhood classroom.

Another point that interested me was that very often the candidates with little if any formal training out-performed those with degrees in early childhood education. Many of the first grade classroom designs were contributed by candidates with degrees in education. Likewise, candidates with extensive training were no more able than candidates with very little training to identify names of children's books or to come up with profound responses to the cartoons.

Analyzing the process

In retrospect I can see that, for me, certain components of the process were more effective than other parts. I found the most instructive part by far was the block building. I learned more about the candidates from this than from all the other components of the process. The next most illuminating part was the personal interview, followed by the cartoon exploration, and then the room design.

I believe that I didn't really begin to tap the great potential of the sentence completions and the autobiographical questions. This is because I lacked the specific skills to reliably interpret the responses in depth. Skilled interviewers and counselors can learn a great deal about persons from these techniques. For example, I showed, anonymously, the sentence completion responses of several candidates we had hired to my independent study adviser at Bank Street College in New York City. From their sentence completions alone she was able to accurately describe a lot about these persons and how they worked with young children. In relation to the autobiographical questions, there is a growing body of research which indicates that people's experiences as children significantly affect how they, as adults, will work with young children. By analyzing a teaching candidate's childhood, a trained counselor can predict what age group of children this person can best work with.

Another conclusion I've reached is that this process could be used effectively to select any type of teacher. For our purposes we looked for candidates who demonstrated openness and creativity in the screening. An employer who was looking for a more structured controlled teacher could use the exact same techniques but look for responses that demonstrated those characteristics. These types of techniques are open and flexible enough to enable any program to attain a successful match between people and program.

This is not to say, of course, that all programs should or could adopt the techniques exactly as I have

described them above. I see what I've done as something very appropriate for me in terms of my interviewing and what I was looking for. I think it is critical that each of us takes a new look at staff selection and designs a process that would be experiential which would allow people to tell us as much as possible about themselves and their abilities. My techniques are simply illustrative of what you might consider. Your own process might incorporate parts of this and it might be totally different. It should include techniques that you feel comfortable with and which enable you to best assess the skills and attitudes that are important to you. Set some time aside and let your creativity loose. A number of persons have made some great adaptations of my process. You can, too!

References

Almy, M. (1975). *The Early Childhood Education at Work.* New York: McGraw Hill Book Company, Chapter 2, "The Early Childhood Educator: An Emerging Role."

Hirsch, Elizabeth S., Ed. (1974). *The Block Book.* Washington, DC: National Association for the Education of Young Children.

Rosen, J. L. (1972). "Matching Teachers with Children." *School Review*, Volume 80, Number 3, pp. 409-431.

Shapiro, E., Biber, B., & Minuchin, P. (1957). "The Cartoons Situation Test:

A Semi-Structured Technique for Assessing Aspects of Personality Pertinent to the Teaching Process," Society for Projective Techniques and Rorschack Institute, Inc.

Yardley, A. (1973). *The Teacher of the Young Child.* New York: Citation Press.

Zimilies, H. (1961). "Teacher Selection and Personality Assessment," *The National Elementary Principal,* Volume 12, Number 2.

Zimilies, H., Biber, B., Rabinowitz, W., & Hay, L. (1964). "Personality Aspects for Teaching: A Predictive Study." *Genetic Psychology Monograms,* Volume 69, pp. 101-149.

Credits

The selection process described in this article was developed as my independent study leading to a Masters of Education in Supervision and Administration of Early Childhood Education at Bank Street College in New York City. Some of the techniques were adapted from matriculation materials developed by the staff at Bank Street College.

Merle W. Leak is currently senior program analyst, day care unit, with the Massachusetts Department of Social Services, and formerly Executive Director of the Bucks County Coordinated Child Care Council.

Selection Interviews: Avoiding the Pitfalls

by Roger Neugebauer

The interview is the most frequently used — and most frequently misused — staff selection tool in early care and education. Nearly all early childhood programs use interviews as a major part, if not the only part, of the process of evaluating the employment suitability of job candidates. Indeed, the interview can provide an employer with useful insights on the qualifications of prospective employees. However, the interview is the most complex of all selection techniques. Centers employing it can encounter any of a number of pitfalls. This article will outline the most frequently encountered pitfalls and will describe techniques for avoiding them.

Pitfall #1

Attempting to assess too much. The interview can be an effective technique for assessing some — but not all — job qualifications. While a candidate's performance in an interview may give a reliable indication of her skills in relating to adults, it sheds little light on her ability to relate to children. To rely solely on an interview to evaluate the suitability of a candidate is placing too much faith in this technique. It is put to best use when used in conjunction with a variety of other techniques such as observations and reference checks.

The interview is most effective in assessing the knowledge, attitudes, and personality of candidates. Even in these areas, however, the interview can only be effective if it is used to assess candidates in terms of a limited number of job qualifications. When interviewers are asked to assess candidates on more than a half dozen factors, they begin to suffer from information overload, and the reliability of their judgment begins to plummet (Shouksmith). Therefore, it is critical at the outset to isolate no more than six key job qualifications to be probed in interviews. It may be helpful to review the full list of qualifications for a job and to distinguish between those which are essential and those which are nice to have but not critical. Then, during the interview, concentrate attention on the "must have" and not on the "nice to have" qualifications (Jensen).

Pitfall #2

Attempting to interview too many candidates. The interviewers had just completed interviewing ten candidates for the position of director in two nights. When they met to select the best candidate, they spent most of their time not objectively weighing the qualifications of each candidate but just trying to unscramble who said what. This incident is not atypical. The more candidates interviewed, the harder it is for interviewers to retain distinct impressions of each of them.

There is, on the other hand, a real advantage in seeing as many candidates in person as possible. This lessens the likelihood of a candidate with the ideal personality for a job falling through the cracks simply because she lacks skills in putting together an impressive resumé. One way to solve this dilemma is to converse with all candidates who possess the minimum job requirements in a brief (five to ten minutes) screening interview.

The purpose of this interview is to outline the nature of the job — its duties, rate of pay, hours, etc. — to the candidate and to secure from the candidate clarification about information on her resumé. From this personal interchange, the interviewer should be able to eliminate from further consideration all candidates whose preparation and/or personality is clearly unsuitable, as well as those who are no longer interested in the job described. The interviewer should also be able to spot those candidates with unimpressive credentials who nonetheless appear to possess the appropriate personality and temperament for the job.

Information overload can also be minimized through judicious scheduling. To give interviewers sufficient opportunity to digest and retain information about candidates interviewed, no more than three interviews should be scheduled for one sitting. Allow 45-60 minutes for each interview, with breaks of at least ten minutes between interviews.

Pitfall #3

Failure to establish rapport. At the outset of an interview, a candidate is likely to be uptight and nervous. Until he relaxes and feels comfortable with talking frankly, he will not present a realistic impression of himself.

Certain details can be arranged to help relieve tension prior to the interview. When the candidate arrives for the interview, he should be made to feel immediately welcome either by having someone greet him or by having a notice posted indicating he is in the right place and that someone will come and get him when it is time for his interview. If there is time, the candidate might be offered a tour of the center.

The candidate should be personally escorted into the interview room and introduced to the interviewers while they are standing. If there is more than one interviewer, the candidate should be seated so that he can easily see all the interviewers, yet not feel like he is on display himself. With one interviewer, both parties should

be seated in comfortable chairs, preferably not on opposite sides of a cluttered desk. After the candidate is seated, there should be a pause which allows him to catch his breath and get his bearings.

To help the candidate *warm up*, an interviewer should get the candidate talking with some easy, non-threatening conversation or questions. This should not be small talk about the weather as this will heighten the tension as the candidate waits for the ax to fall. The interviewer could start with some point of common interest from the resumé — "I went to North Dakota State also. How did you like it there?" — or with a series of specific, easy-to-answer questions. Do not rush this phase of the interview as the interchange will not be open and frank until rapport has been established. Then once you are ready to begin in earnest, brief the candidate on what the interview will be like so he knows what to expect.

Pitfall #4

Having too many interviewers. The most common pitfall in child care selection interviews is the *Spanish Inquisition* syndrome — bringing candidates before a panel of four to ten inquisitors. It is hard enough for a single interviewer to establish rapport with a candidate. When there are two or more interviewers, it becomes much more difficult, and when there are four or more, it is usually impossible. As a result, there is "a loss of sense of intimacy, a diminution of empathy, a confused interviewer, and a consequent inhibition of communication" (Lopez). In a panel interview setting, it is also much more difficult to proceed in an organized fashion, to carry out a line of questioning to completion, and to ask spontaneous follow-up questions.

There are, nonetheless, occasions when, for either political or programmatic reasons, it is necessary to have more than one interviewer. An alternative to consider in these situations is the serial interview whereby one candidate is interviewed by a number of interviewers individually in sequence. Each interviewer covers different job qualifications or aspects of the job. In the end, all interviewers meet to share their impressions and findings.

Pitfall #5

Failure to provide enough structure. Research on selection interviews has uncovered many shortcomings of informal, unstructured interviews: They are highly inconsistent and highly susceptible to distortion and bias (Pursell); the same materials are not covered for all candidates; interviewers tend to talk more than interviewees; and interviewers tend to make their decisions early in the interview (Stewart). In addition, interviewers tend to spend more time formulating their next question than listening to what the candidate is saying (Goodale).

For best results, most personnel experts recommend a well-prepared for, semi-structured interview format. Prior to the interview, the key job qualifications to be probed in the interview should be identified, and one or two open-ended introductory questions should be developed for each qualification. After the interview has progressed through the rapport-building stage, the interviewer should introduce a job qualification with one of these open-ended questions, and then follow up with specific spontaneous questions which seek clarification of issues raised in the candidate's initial response.

Pitfall #6

Being swayed by general impressions and stereotypes. Interviewers often are struck by a single aspect of a candidate's personality or background or by a single statement and allow this single factor to determine their overall assessment of the candidate. For example, the physical appearance of a candidate, especially one who is very thin, fat, short, tall, good looking, well dressed, or poorly dressed, will often color an interviewer's judgment about a candidate (Jensen). Interviewers also tend to be influenced more by unfavorable information revealed by a candidate than by favorable information; and the earlier in the interview the unfavorable information is disclosed, the greater its negative impact (Stewart).

To keep such biases and distortions from undermining the selection process, interviewers need to be encouraged to concentrate on gathering specific pieces of relevant evidence about candidates' qualifications, rather than general impressions. One way to do this is to spend some time prior to the interviews reviewing the job qualifications so that interviewers are well aware of what information to probe for. A second approach is to provide training on effective listening skills (see Nichols).

Pitfall #7

Failure to record information. By the end of an interview, interviewers generally have already forgotten 50% of what was said. By the next day, 85% has been forgotten (Nichols). Therefore, even though it may be somewhat distracting or discomforting to the candidate, it is critical to record information during the interview.

The best method is to tape record interviews. When doing this, tell candidates at the outset that the interview will be taped and for what purpose. A candidate may feel uptight with being recorded, but generally after the first few minutes everyone tends to forget about the recorder and converse normally.

The next best method is to take notes onto a format prepared in advance which provides spaces for each qualification. When taking notes, however, it is necessary to avoid telegraphing what you want to hear by stopping to write whenever the candidate says something of interest. Instead, the interviewer should make a mental note of valuable points and record these when attention shifts to another interviewer or point in the discussion. In either case, after the interviews, the interviewers should take a few minutes to record their reactions.

Pitfall #8

Asking discriminatory questions. Interviewers are barred by equal employment opportunity guidelines from asking questions that can lead to discrimination on the basis of race, religion, age, sex, marital status, arrest record, handicaps, or national origin. Questions such as the following are not legal:

- Do you live with your parents?

- Who will watch your children while you work?

- How do you get along with other women?

- Do you have any physical disabilities?

- Where were you born?

- Have you ever been arrested?

- How would you feel about working with people younger than yourself?

- Does your religion prevent you from working weekends?

This does not mean, however, that no questions can be asked about these subjects. They can be asked in reference to bona-fide occupational qualifications. For example, although a candidate cannot be asked "Are you

More Dos and Don'ts for Selection Interviews

- To encourage a candidate to be open, praise her for answering questions fully.

- To be sure you understand a candidate or to probe for more details, restate what she told you, but in an expectant tone — "You say you have had difficulty working with aggressive parents. . . ."

- Use silence to draw candidates out. People tend to be uncomfortable with silence in a conversation. When a candidate stops talking but has not supplied enough details on a point, don't rush to fill the void. Wait for the candidate to speak up.

- Don't do all the talking. The more you talk, the less you learn.

- Don't ask questions which are answered in the resumé.

- Don't telegraph what you want to hear by describing the philosophy of the center at the outset or by asking leading questions — "Do you believe in open education?"

- Don't reveal your reactions or feelings either through gestures, expressions, or remarks. This may cause the candidate to clam up or tailor her remarks to suit you.

- Don't debate issues with the candidate or seek to give advice.

- Don't ask trick questions. You cannot encourage the candidate to be open and frank if you are being devious yourself.

- Don't rely on general questions about teaching philosophies. How a candidate describes her approach in theory and how she performs in practice often bear little resemblance. Specific situational questions — "What would you do if . . ." — may be more instructive.

- Don't allow the interview to get sidetracked on an interesting but non-job-related tangent.

- Don't let the candidate take control of the interview.

- Don't allow the candidate to sense your impatience.

candidate in the batch if that candidate is so turned off by the image the organization conveyed during the selection process that she turns down the job offer.

Throughout the interview process, all candidates should be treated warmly and professionally. Appointments should be clearly made and adhered to. Candidates should be made to feel welcome when they arrive and respected when they depart. Having a well-structured interview not only yields more information about the candidates, it also shows the candidates that they are dealing with a professional organization and that the organization takes the job under consideration seriously.

Near the end of the interview, time should be set aside for describing the organization and the job to the candidate. Questions from the candidate should be welcomed at this point also. In describing the job and answering questions about it, however, care should be taken not to oversell it. If there are negative aspects of the job (low pay, a split shift, or a recent history of staff turmoil), these should be discussed with candidates. The interview should be viewed as the first step in negotiating a contract. A new employee's commitment to the center may be seriously undermined if the center can't deliver on promises made or expectations aroused in the interview.

a U.S. citizen?," the question "Can you, after employment, submit verification of your legal right to work in the United States?" is acceptable (Jensen). Centers which are uncertain about the legality of their selection procedures should contact their state's Equal Opportunity Commission.

Pitfall #9

Failure to sell the organization to the candidate. Interviewers can become so preoccupied with assessing the candidates that they may not be aware of the impression they are making on the candidate. It is counterproductive to select the best

At the close of the interview, the candidate should be told the process that will follow and when and how she will be notified of the decision. Unless a candidate clearly lacks some basic job qualification, no indication should be given at this time about whether or not the candidate is likely to get the job.

References

Goodale, J. G. (July 1981). "The Neglected Art of Interviewing." *Supervisory Management.*

Jensen, J. (May/June 1981). "How to Hire the Right Person for the Job." *The Grantsmanship Center News.*

Lopez, F. M. (1965). *Personnel Interviewing: Theory and Practice.* New York: McGraw-Hill Book Company.

Nichols, R. G. (November 1980). "Improve Your Listening Skills." *Exchange.*

Pursell, E. D. (November 1980). "Structured Interviewing: Avoiding Selection Problems." *Personnel Journal.*

Shouksmith, G. (1968). *Assessment Through Interviewing.* Oxford, England: Pergamon Press, Ltd.

Stewart, C. J., & Cash, W. B. (1974). *Interviewing: Principles and Practices.* Dubuque, IA: William C. Brown Company, Publishers.

Observing Teaching Candidates in Action

by Roger Neugebauer

"We found that everyone loves children in the abstract, but will they love them eight hours a day in the classroom?" Thus Nancy Alexander explained the reason her center in Shreveport, Louisiana, instituted a policy of observing all teaching candidates before they were hired. At first, when teachers were selected strictly on the basis of their performance, she found that there often was a wide variance between how individuals described their child caring skills and how they actually performed in action. By observing likely candidates working in a center, Nancy Alexander was able to much more reliably assess them. As a result, she nearly eliminated hiring mistakes.

This experience is not unique. Most early care and education programs now include observations as an integral part of their selection procedures. To provide readers with ideas on how to conduct an effective observation, *Exchange* surveyed eight early care and education organizations which have experienced positive results with this staff selection technique. The results of this survey are summarized below.

Before the observation

An observation can provide a reasonably reliable forecast of a candidate's likely performance if it is properly prepared for. This preparation should center around the identification of what you hope to learn about candidates in the observations.

You probably can generate a long list of qualifications you would like to find in your ideal teaching candidate. Some of these, such as *level of training*, can be reliably measured by a resumé review; and others, such as *knowledge of child development*, can be assessed well in interviews. Many others, especially those relating to personality traits and teaching style, can only be assessed by observing the candidates in action. Identify about a half dozen of these qualifications or traits that are most critical to the accomplishment of your center's curriculum goals. Don't attempt to assess too many or your attention will be dispersed in too many directions to effectively measure anything.

For each trait, identify some specific indicators to look for during the observation. For example, if an important qualification is *positive interaction skills*, helpful indicators of this might be *maintains eye contact at the child's level* and *listens patiently to children*. At the end of this article are listed 29 such indicators that the surveyed directors found to yield insightful data on the candidates.

Thoroughly discuss the list of qualifications and their indicators in a staff meeting. Make sure that anyone who will participate in observations understands what to look for. Make any revisions that come out of this discussion for improving or clarifying the list. Then print it up in a checklist format to hand to observers before each observation to be sure the traits and indicators are attended to.

With this degree of preparation, observation can be a more reliable staff selection technique than the interview. It would be desirable to be able to observe all candidates who meet the center's minimum training and experience standards. This might enable you to identify candidates who don't have impressive formal qualifications and who do not express themselves skillfully in the interview but who, nevertheless, are naturally gifted in interacting with children. Unfortunately, observations are time consuming and a bit disruptive to the flow of classroom activities. Therefore, most centers tend to use observations sparingly — only observing the top two to five candidates from the interviews. If this is the approach your center must take, follow your hunches from time to time. Include among those to be observed candidates who didn't fare well through the interview stage but who you have a gut feeling may do well in practice.

Bea Ganson, a director in Abilene, Texas, is able to get a maximum use of observations by requiring all candidates to serve as paid substitutes before they can be hired. Thus she can observe many candidates over a period of time before making selection decisions.

During the observation

One teaching candidate, upon inquiring at a center about a job, was immediately assigned for his *observation* to care for 15 children in the nap room by himself. Many of the children could not be comforted by this *stranger*, and most of the others took the opportunity to test him. The result was chaos. The candidate had a miserable experience and never considered returning to that center, and the center didn't get the foggiest picture of what the candidate was like as a teacher.

For the best results, the center should schedule observations carefully. Centers have found that observations should last at least two to four hours to get a reliable picture of a candidate. Shorter periods do not allow candidates enough time to get acclimated.

Time of day is also critical. Nancy Alexander schedules interviews during a free play period rather than a group activity time so that candidates are more likely to get involved with the children rather than sitting

back and observing an activity. Peg Persinger, a director in Eugene, Oregon, tends to assign candidates to the most challenging groups to really test their skills. Most directors also assign candidates to work with teachers they would actually be working with if they were hired, so that the current teachers can assess whether this is someone they would be comfortable with.

In any event, try to have all candidates for a single position be observed by the same staff people. Barbara Day, a director in Edmonton, Alberta, recommends scheduling all observations for a single position in the same week so that the memories of the first candidates won't fade by the time the last ones are observed.

For the candidate to present a true picture of herself, she needs to be as relaxed and comfortable as possible. For the candidate to be interested in working for the center, she needs to have as pleasant an experience as possible. Both these requirements call for the director to take specific steps to put the candidate at ease about the observation and to ease her into it gently. Start by telling all candidates from the beginning that they may be expected to participate in an observation. When scheduling interviews, tell them exactly what will be expected of them, how long the observation will last, and what the class is like that they will be in.

On the day of the observation, the director should escort the candidate into the room and introduce her to the teaching staff and the children. At this point, Barbara Day leaves the candidate, and the supervisor (or head teacher) leads the candidate on a brief tour of the room.

The candidate's involvement in the activity of the room should be allowed to expand gradually. Most centers allow for a 30 minute *warm-up* period in which no official obser-

vations are made. Candidates under observation at the North Pocono Preschool in North Pocono, Pennsylvania, are encouraged by director Gail Laskowski to start their four hour observation by observing what is going on for a while, then working with the teachers for a while, and finally working on their own when they feel comfortable doing so.

Many centers ask the candidates to plan and present a specific 20-40 minute activity for the children. Karen Miller, Evergreen, Colorado, has found that if some of the less experienced candidates are not given such a specific task, they tend to sit around, giving no hint of their potential. Staff should go out of their way to cooperate with the candidates in providing materials and assistance for the activities. Give the candidates every opportunity to do their best.

During the observation, it is best not to heighten their sense of being followed by all eyes. The director should not pull up a chair and formally observe the whole period. Gail Laskowski simply makes a point of being in the area with a purpose often during this period. The teachers should also go on about their business and not take notes or talk about the candidate in her presence.

On the other hand, the staff should not ignore the candidate but should be alert to her performance. While observers should take note of a candidate's general demeanor, they should most keenly observe how he handles specific incidents. The data they should be trying to collect is not general impressions but as many small pieces of evidence as possible — especially pieces of evidence relating to the indicators identified beforehand.

After the observation

There should be a definite closure to the observation. The director should return to the room to retrieve the candidate, or the head teacher should thank her and ask her to report back to the director. At this point, Barbara Day invites the candidate to share her reactions. These reactions can be very revealing. The candidate's impressions of specific incidents can disclose a great deal about her knowledge and philosophy. For example, the candidate may talk about the *misbehavior* of a certain *troublemaker* when in reality this child's behavior was well within normal bounds. This may be a clue to you that either this candidate is not tuned in to child development or else that she may have a more restrictive approach than you prefer. If the candidate shares only general reactions, it may be useful to prod her memory with open-ended statements about specific incidents.

After the candidate leaves, all those who observed her should take the first opportunity to record their reactions. Gail Laskowski has all observers rate the candidate on a selection criteria matrix and then include some narrative comments. Then, as soon as possible, while the experience is still fresh in everyone's minds, the observers should meet together to share their assessments. The director should steer this discussion away from generalities. One way to do this is to read through the list of traits and their indicators. For each indicator, ask observers to describe specific incidents where this indicator was demonstrated in a negative or positive way. If the indicator relates to the candidate's success in integrating children into the group, the observers would describe a candidate's various attempts to do so and the outcome of the attempts. By reviewing as much specific evidence as possible, the observers will eventually have a reasonably solid basis for deciding whether or not to hire the candidate.

Observations can add a strong element of reliability to staff selection decisions. However, this technique does not guarantee that all mistakes will be avoided. Charlene Richardson, director of the Child Development Center in San Diego, places new employees on a three month probationary status. During this period, she carefully monitors their performance using the same procedures as in the selection observation. Such pre- and post-hiring observations do require considerable effort on the part of staff members; but in the long run, they assure a more consistent program for the children.

What to look for

The directors surveyed for this article identified the following performance indicators as ones they have used with the best results. Overall, the indicators that were cited most frequently related to the way the candidates relate to the children. As Nancy Alexander explained, "We want to see if they treat them as sweet cutesies or as thinking human beings." In this vein, the most popular indicators were tone of voice, eye contact, body language, and listening skills.

Physical appearance and personal attitude

- Does she use positive body language?

- Is her tone of voice appropriate?

- What are her facial expressions as she interacts with children? Is she animated, angry, or "bored to tears"?

- Does she maintain eye contact at the child's level?

- Does she dress appropriately, "as if she expects to sit on the floor and have tempera paint spilled over her?"

- Does she convey an overall sense of enthusiasm?

- Is she having fun or is she tense and resentful?

Interaction skills

- How does she react when children approach her?

- How does she answer children's questions?

- Does she listen carefully and patiently to what children tell her? How does she signal interest in their communications?

- Does she appear comfortable talking to children?

- Does she serve as a good language model?

- How does she help integrate children into the group?

Direction and control

- Does she maintain control? How?

- How does she show tolerance for child-like demands, impatience, mood swings, self-assertion, negativism, exuberance, angry feelings, tears, and testing behavior? How does she guide children at such times toward adequate coping and socially acceptable behavior?

- Does she allow children to resolve their own conflicts?

- How much are children allowed to diverge from her directions?

- If a child has lost control, can the candidate accept the child's feelings and help him regain control? Does she retaliate or offer alternatives? Does she tear the child down or build him up?

- Does the candidate use a positive approach — "Blocks are for building." — or are her directives negative — "Don't throw that block."

Teaching skills

- Is she actively engaged or merely babysitting?

- If she brings in an activity, is it appropriate for the age group?

- Is she able to follow a schedule while still remaining flexible?

- Is she able to adjust to unforeseen incidents?

- How well does she hold the interest of the children?

- How well does she arouse children's curiosity?

- Does she move around the room to help children and show interest in what they are doing?

- Does she provide an appropriate balance of unstructured and structured activities?

- Does she demonstrate a willingness to learn herself? Is she open to new ideas? Does she ask questions about particular activities and materials?

- Does she work comfortably with other staff in the room?

Chapter 2

Developing Personnel Policies
and
Procedures

An Ounce of Prevention: How to Write an Employee Handbook

by Joe Perreault and Roger Neugebauer

Hopefully your employee handbook will be the best written document you never use.

In an ideal world, you and your employees will work in perfect harmony, with communication flowing back and forth unhindered and work being performed in an exemplary fashion. In this dream world, your employee handbook will gather dust on the shelf.

In the real world, however, even the best-intentioned director is going to encounter frustration, anger, and disappointment in working with others. You may fail to clearly explain all center rules and procedures to a new employee, or exhibit poor judgment in denying a raise to an old employee. Teachers may arrive late, take shortcuts with health procedures, or make inappropriate remarks to parents.

In the real world, you and your staff periodically will need to refer to an employee handbook to resolve disputes and miscommunications. A well-conceived employee handbook helps soften these bumps and grinds by 1) spelling out what types of behavior are encouraged and discouraged and 2) informing employees about their rights and benefits.

In this article, we will provide some pointers on overall organizational issues such as content, the development process, design, and writing style of an employee handbook.

Cover the waterfront

An employee handbook should be more than just a listing of rules and rewards. It should serve as a one-stop source of answers to any questions that might arise regarding one's employment. The sample table of contents included in this article demonstrates the range of issues that some centers include in an employee handbook.

In reviewing dozens of personnel documents developed by child care centers, we noted that their most common weakness content-wise was a failure to provide employees with a sense of the history and mission of the organization. At a minimum, an employee handbook should open with a statement of the goals or philosophy of the organization. Such introductory comments provide an important framework for all the rules and procedures that follow.

Manuals that provided the broadest array of information even pulled together descriptions of center routines — procedures for health and safety, problem solving, field trips, emergencies, abuse reporting, grievances, telephone answering, and center visits. Having all such procedures located in one place makes it easier to find than if they are scattered about on various memos and bulletin boards.

Reach out for ideas

No matter who makes the final decisions on personnel policies and procedures — whether it be an owner, a board of directors, or a center director — these decisions will be improved if ideas from a variety of perspectives are scrutinized during the development process.

Obviously, employees affected by these decisions can offer valuable insights. Their opinions on the fairness of policies and procedures should be considered before decisions are made. In addition, their opinions on whether the writing is comprehensible are important. If procedures are described poorly, they will not be followed. The fact that a procedure makes sense to the person writing it up is not a measure of how well it will be understood by those who have to carry it out.

It is also useful to do some brainstorming about what needs to be included in an employee handbook. You might ask every member of the organization (teachers, substitutes, cooks, secretaries, and janitors) to write down five "what if" questions that the handbook should answer. For example, people might ask, "What happens if I have sick leave left at the end of the year?" or "What happens if a snowstorm hits in the middle of the day?" or "What happens if a newspaper reporter calls for an interview?"

It may also be stimulating to take a look at the personnel manuals of other child care centers. This might give you some alternatives to consider on thorny policy questions, as well as some ideas on content and design. However, you should avoid borrowing policies word for word from other manuals without modifying them to fit your unique circumstances.

You should also have a lawyer review your handbook before it is printed. He will need to check whether your policies and procedures are in compliance with applicable laws. He might also provide useful advice on whether what you propose is too vague or cumbersome, and whether you are leaving yourself enough flexibility.

Finally, you should have someone who knows your organization very well review your handbook to see if it consistently reflects the style and values of your organization. If your management style is firm and authoritative, your employee handbook shouldn't sound like it was written by Abbey Hoffman.

Likewise, if you run a freewheeling, do-your-own-thing operation, your handbook shouldn't read like the Marine Corps' drill sergeants' rule book. The dissonance between what you say in writing and what you do in real life will confuse and frustrate employees.

Make it user friendly

Research by the American Management Association found that the major criticisms of employee handbooks by users are problems in finding information, and in understanding what is said. The way a handbook is organized and written will in large measure determine if it helps or hinders the supervisory process. Here are some suggestions for ensuring that the messages you want to convey in a handbook are communicated:

- Start with a detailed table of contents. An employee with a question on reimbursement for travel expenses shouldn't have to wade through the sections on benefits, attendance, and compensation in order to find an answer. She should be able to find out where to look in the table of contents.

- Number pages consecutively throughout. In other words, don't start numbering over with each section (A1, A2, A3 . . . B1, B2, B3 . . . C1, C2, C3, etc.). This type of numbering makes it easy for editors who need to insert frequent updates, but it is user hostile. How can you turn quickly to page E23?

- If your handbook is more than 20 pages long, consider using some device to visually differentiate major sections. Print each chapter on differently colored paper or use chapter dividers with plastic tabs. Find the book *A Sign of Relief* (New York: Bantam Books, 1984) and see the devices it uses to help make its first-aid information quickly accessible.

- Make it easy on the eyes. Have your final product printed on a letter-quality printer. Choose an easy-to-read type font. Leave plenty of white space on every page. If your resources are limited, spend your money on high quality printing rather than on fancy paper or deluxe binders.

- Don't make it cumbersome to read. The personnel documents we reviewed were printed in all shapes, sizes, and formats. Of all of these, two set-ups seemed to work best. Letter-sized sheets, three-hole punched, to go in a three-ring binder were our first choice. In this format, the pages lie flat — you don't have to hold the pages down to keep from losing your place; updated pages can be easily replaced; and you can insert other center documents in the same binder for convenience.

Our second choice was letter-sized sheets stapled together in the upper left-hand corner. This format worked

Typical Contents of an Employee Handbook

I. **Introduction**
    A. Table of contents
    B. How to use this handbook
    C. How the handbook is updated

II. **Welcome to Hippety Hop Child Care Center**
    A. History of Hippety Hop Child Care Center
    B. Philosophy of Hippety Hop Child Care Center
    C. Goals and mission statement of Hippety Hop Child Care Center
    D. Organizational structure of Hippety Hop Child Care Center

III. **Terms of Employment**
    A. Categories of employment (i.e., permanent full time, permanent part time, temporary part time, probationary, substitute, etc.)
    B. Job descriptions
    C. Hiring (posting vacancies, screening procedures, hiring of relatives, physical exams and other pre-employment requirements, and non-discrimination statement)
    D. Compensation (salary plan, timekeeping, pay periods, pay days, overtime)
    E. Supervision and evaluation
    F. Discipline and termination
    G. Voluntary resignation
    H. Grievance procedures

IV. **Expectations of Employees**
    A. Attendance (hours, absenteeism, lateness, inclement weather days)
    B. Staff development (participation in meetings, planning, and training)
    C. Interactions with children (guidelines for interactions with, and discipline of, children)
    D. Interactions with adults (guidelines for written, in person, or telephone communication with parents, staff, board members, visitors, media representatives, vendors, and public officials)
    E. Problem solving procedures
    F. Health and safety procedures
    G. Field trip procedures
    H. Emergency procedures
    I. Reporting requirements (injuries and accidents, suspicion of abuse, safety concerns)
    J. Other requirements (outside employment, dress, eating, smoking, telephoning, leaving premises)

V. **Benefits for Employees**
    A. Time off (holidays, vacations, personal leave, sick leave, jury duty, parenting leave, disability leave, leave without pay)
    B. Bonuses and awards
    C. Insurance (health, life, dental, Social Security, workers' compensation, unemployment, etc.)
    D. Other benefits (breaks, meals, uniforms, travel reimbursement, tuition assistance, reductions in child care fees, retirement plans, etc.)

well for shorter documents because pages can easily be turned. If you choose this format, it works best to print only on one side of the page.

- Use consistent formatting for all center documents — parent handbooks, operations manuals, curriculum guides, business plans. All your documents will be easier to access if the same formatting, style, and organizational logic is followed. This also lends a more professional tone to your efforts, and gives them more credibility.

- Write like you talk. Just because you are writing a manual doesn't mean you have to lapse into unintelligible bureaucratize. After you write a paragraph, read it out loud. If it sounds stilted and clumsy as you talk it, that's how it's going to come across to someone reading it.

- Make it lively. Inject zest into your writing by leading off with a punch, attending to the cadence of your sentences, and sticking to active, colorful words.

- Make the organization abundantly clear. Use headlines and subheads as a road map for the reader to guide him to the exact information he wants as directly as possible.

- Don't sound like a nag. No one enjoys being beat over the head with page after page of rules and restrictions. Set a positive tone by opening with an upbeat summary of the strengths and goals of your organization. Stress the positive environment you are striving to establish for parents, staff, and children. Wherever possible, state your policies and procedures in terms of the positive behaviors to be emulated, rather than the negative behaviors to be avoided.

Create a living document

Writing an employee handbook is hard work, plenty of hard work. You don't want to go to all this trouble if the handbook is going to fall into disuse in six months. Make sure your work stands the test of time by making it easy to update. Here are some suggestions:

- The best way to extend the life of any manual is to develop and store it on a computer. That way, when sections require revision, all you have to do is bring up the portions in question on your computer, make the necessary changes, and print out the new version of the page, chapter, or section.

- Whenever you make a change to the handbook, replace at least an entire page. Don't circulate attachments or appendices intended to supersede sections that remain in the manual. Such updates are messy and confusing.

- Enter the effective date on the bottom of every page in your handbook. This minimizes confusion as to which is the current information.

- Do not include in the body of your handbook information that changes frequently or which is explained in detail elsewhere. Package your handbook in a binder with front and back pockets.

A final caution

An employee handbook is not the cure-all for employee headaches. Having policies and procedures spelled out clearly in writing doesn't guarantee that they will be carried out.

Look upon the handbook as one means of communicating the policies, procedures, and priorities of the center to employees. To ensure that all staff are performing appropriately, you need to supplement written guidance with an active orientation, ongoing staff development, and responsible supervision and monitoring.

A well-written employee handbook is an important cornerstone of an effective supervisory process. It sets sights, clarifies expectations, and establishes ground rules. Hopefully, all other components of the supervisory process will work so well that this handbook will seldom be used.

Developing Your Employee Handbook: Leave Policies

by Joe Perreault and Roger Neugebauer

In developing your center's employee handbook, you are continually striving to reconcile the personal needs of employees with the day-to-day realities of operating your center. No section of your handbook better exemplifies this balancing act than the policies regarding time away from work.

All workers need opportunities to restore their physical and emotional health and to deal with personal and civic responsibilities. At the same time, in order to provide a quality service, an early childhood program needs to maintain a high level of continuity in its staffing. The center's leave policies should, therefore, seek to fulfill employees' need for time off in a way that maintains a consistent staffing pattern.

Finding the right balance is not easy. Since no two centers share exactly the same mix of resources, goals, educational philosophies, and management styles, there is no ideal set of leave policies that will work in every center. In fact, in reviewing employee handbooks from over 50 early childhood organizations in preparing this article, we found over 50 unique versions of leave policies.

In this article, we will outline for you the many choices that you will need to make — the questions you will need to answer — in molding leave policies to meet the needs of your center. In addition, we will share examples of the varied policies that centers have adopted. (Note: Centers whose leave policies are cited are listed at the end of this article. We have not credited excerpts specifically since, taken out of context, they may not fairly reflect a center's overall posture.)

Vacation leave

How much vacation time should be offered? Centers typically grant full-time employees between five and ten days of vacation time per year, with the average closer to ten days. The number of days granted increases as employees accrue years of service, usually at the rate of one additional day per year.

Should part-time and temporary employees be granted vacations? Some centers grant vacation time only to full-time employees. However, as it is becoming harder to recruit qualified staff, more centers are offering such benefits to help attract solid part-time staff. Often vacation time for part-time staff is granted in proportion to hours worked. For example, a teacher working half time would be granted one half the vacation time of full-time teachers.

When can vacation time be taken? For new teachers, there is often a probationary period during which vacation time cannot be taken. Typically this waiting period is 90 days but extends as long as six months in some centers. In most centers, new teachers still accrue vacation credit during this period.

Most centers require that time taken off for vacations be approved in advance, and some even restrict the times during which these vacations can be taken. Some examples:

Vacations shall be planned for the mutual convenience of the staff and the center. In deciding preferences for vacation time, the primary consideration will be the necessary coverage of the center's services. Otherwise, position and seniority of service, as well as mutual agreement among staff, will be considered. Requests for vacation should be made at least one month in advance in writing. These requests will be granted on a first requested, first received basis. No more than two employees in each group may take a vacation at any one time. Employees are encouraged to spread their vacations throughout the year and cooperate in planning their vacations so that everyone may use the periods best suited to their needs.

Vacation must be taken at Christmas time or between June 1 and August 15.

Can vacation time be used in advance or, conversely, not used and carried over from year to year? Most centers require that vacation time must be earned before it is used and that it must be used in the same year that it is earned. Some centers allow time to be carried over, and some even provide that employees can be paid for unused leave upon termination. Frequently, directors have authority to grant exceptions in unusual circumstances. Some examples:

Vacation leave is to be utilized on a yearly basis based upon anniversary of employment. Leave not utilized by anniversary date must be forfeited.

Unused vacation leave may be carried over to the following year to a five day maximum. Accumulated vacation pay, up to a limit of two weeks, may be paid upon termination of satisfactory service if notice is received two weeks in advance.

How will vacation time be calculated? To avoid confusion and disputes, the method of calculating how much leave an employee has earned should be spelled out clearly. It is recommended that this method be as simple as possible. (These points apply equally to all forms of leave.) For example, some centers grant one half day of leave at the end of each pay period. Others credit the employee with one or two days of leave at the end of every full month of service completed by the employee.

Sick leave

How much time off for sickness should be offered? Centers typically offer full-time employees from seven to twelve days of sick leave per year. Some offer sick leave to part-time employees on a prorated basis. One center offers sick leave to all employees "... at the rate of one hour earned for every 21 hours worked."

For what purposes can sick leave be used? Most centers restrict the use of sick leave to instances where the employee is physically unable to perform. Other centers allow it to be used more flexibly. Some examples:

Sick leave may be approved for personal illness or injury, for an employee who is required to take care of an illness in one's immediate family, or for an employee who has been exposed to a contagious disease which might endanger fellow employees or children.

Sick leave may be used for illness of the employee, illness of a minor child residing in the employee's home, for a doctor's appointment which cannot be scheduled during off hours, in the event of a death or serious illness in the immediate family, and for absence due to pregnancy.

How will the appropriate use of sick leave be verified? Many centers insert language and procedures into employee handbooks to protect

against the abuse of sick leave. Many require an employee to notify one's supervisor in advance of using sick leave and to provide a doctor's verification of illness for extended periods of leave. Some examples:

An employee who will be absent shall notify the director before scheduled starting time on the first day of illness (or the night before if possible) and each successive day. Request for sick leave for a medical, dental, or optical examination shall be submitted to the director as far in advance as possible.

Approval of sick leave is not automatic. An employee requesting sick leave must notify his/her supervisor of the nature and expected duration of the illness or injury. Employees must keep their supervisor informed about their condition and the probable date of their return to work. Employees who do not keep their supervisor so informed are subject to disciplinary action or termination.

Any employee missing work for health, mental, or emotional reasons can be required by the supervisor to supply a doctor's statement confirming the condition and/or the recovery. The supervisor, not the doctor, has the responsibility and authority to determine if an employee is sufficiently recovered to return to work and if the doctor's written confirmation is sufficient to justify sick leave being authorized.

Any unapproved sick leave taken on the day preceding or following a center holiday shall result in no pay for the holiday itself.

It must be expressly understood that excessive time out for sickness hurts the quality of our program and, therefore, cannot be permitted. If, in the director's judgment, an employee's absences are excessive, counseling, probation, and/or termination with cause will result.

Can sick leave be used in advance or, conversely, not used and carried over from year to year? Most centers provide the director with the authority to grant sick leave in advance when circumstances merit. In addition, most centers allow employees to accumulate sick leave and carry it over from year to year (this practice is more common than allowing employees to carry over annual leave). The amount of sick leave that can be accumulated ranges from 20 to 132 days, with most falling in the 30 to 50 day range. About half the centers surveyed pay staff members for unused sick leave upon termination.

Personal leave

In recent years, there has been a movement toward personal leave. This is a catch-all leave category that employees can use for personal reasons that don't fit into any other leave categories. Some centers grant vacation leave, sick leave, and personal leave; other centers grant vacation leave and personal leave; and some centers have gone so far as to consolidate all leave into one overall personal leave category designed to cover the entire range of an employee's needs for time off.

Proponents of personal leave argue that it sets up a more professional relationship with employees. They are no longer required to play the *calling in sick* game, or dip into precious vacation leave, when what they really need to do is care for a sick family member, entertain visiting relatives, meet with their lawyer, or take a day away from work to restore their emotional energy.

Opponents, on the other hand, argue that loosening leave policies in this way encourages employees to take more days off. These fears tend to be misplaced. Personnel studies have consistently shown that the amount of time off that employees take is much more dependent upon their satisfaction with their work environ-ment than it is upon the strictness of the leave policies. In other words, employees who are unhappy with their jobs will take as much time off as they can, and employees who are highly motivated will take little time off.

Leave without pay

Under what circumstances will an employee be granted leave without pay? There are two general categories for leave without pay — voluntary and involuntary. Voluntary leave without pay applies when an employee needs to take time off for an extended period and does not have enough vacation or sick leave to cover this time. In this category, centers typically include leave for serious illness, pregnancy, education, or other urgent personal reasons.

Involuntary leave without pay is charged when an employee is absent from work without authorization (for example, if an employee failed to show up for work and didn't call in ahead of time as required by center policies) or when the director determines that the employee is unable to carry out his/her responsibilities (for example, if an employee was ill or injured).

What restrictions apply? Many centers restrict leave without pay to full-time employees who have been with the center for a minimum period of time. This time period ranges from six months to two years. Centers usually require that the employee request such leave 30 to 180 days in advance in order for the center to find a replacement. Some centers place a limit of anywhere from three months to two years on the length of a leave of absence.

What benefits does an employee retain while on leave without pay? In most cases, employees on leave without pay status do not accrue annual leave or sick leave, nor do they earn credit toward length of service salary increments. Some centers specifically state that an authorized leave without pay will not constitute a break in service in determining continuing eligibility for seniority and the retirement plan.

Some centers maintain the employee's medical insurance coverage up to three to six months, while others require that the employee bear the full cost of premiums in order to maintain coverage while on leave. An employee placed on leave without pay due to a job-related disability may be eligible for compensation under the Workers' Compensation Act.

Is the employee guaranteed a job upon return? Centers tend to be guarded in the language they use in this area:

If during your leave of absence it becomes necessary to fill your position, we will make every effort to return you to a similar position at a similar hourly rate. However, we cannot guarantee that a position will be available.

Other forms of leave

Jury duty. Centers allow employees time off with pay when they are summoned to serve on a jury. A typical policy reads:

Employees called for jury duty will be paid the difference between their regular base salary and the amount received as compensation for jury duty. A copy of the summons must be presented to your supervisor as soon as it is received. The center reserves the right to request an exemption from jury duty for an employee. No leave is charged for jury duty.

Military leave. Federal law requires that employers provide employees leave for certain forms of military service. One center's policy:

Employees who present official orders requiring attendance for a period of active military duty will be entitled to military leave with full pay, less that paid for military service, for a period not to exceed two weeks.

Bereavement leave. Most centers grant employees up to three days of leave with pay to attend the funeral of an employee's or spouse's immediate family member (spouse, children, sister, brother, parent, grandparent).

A final caution

The purpose of this article was to outline the range of choices you should address when developing your center's leave policies. Since labor laws vary in all states and localities, this was not intended to provide legal advice. Before adopting your policies, you should have your lawyer review them in terms of applicable local, state, and federal labor laws. While centers have a great deal of latitude in the policies they develop, in certain areas — such as maternity leave, disability, jury duty, and military leave — legal restrictions will apply.

Sources of examples

Central Learning and Day Care Center, Memphis, TN; Child Care Center, Evanston, IL; Child Inc., Austin, TX; Children's World Learning Centers, Golden, CO; Day Nursery Association, Indianapolis, IN; Episcopal Child Day Care Centers, Jacksonville, FL; Handicapped Children's Association, Johnson City, NY; Ithaca Child Care Center, Ithaca, NY; Jane Addams Day Care Center, Toms River, NJ; Janet Rich Day Care Center, Rochester, NY; Mercy Child Development Center, Des Moines, IA; Mercyhurst Child Care Center, Erie, PA; Moffett Road Baptist Child Development Center, Mobile, AL; Neighborhood Centers Association, Houston, TX; Nursery Foundation, St. Louis, MO; Ohio State University Child Care Center, Columbus, OH; Playcare Child Care Centers, Rochester, NY; Presbyterian Child Development Center, Wellsboro, PA; Rainbow Chimes, Huntington, NY; Reston Children's Center, Reston, VA; Summit Child Care Center, Summit, NJ; The Learning Center, Jackson, WY; and United Day Care Services, Greensboro, NC.

Developing the Employee Handbook: Grievance Procedure

by Joe Perreault and Roger Neugebauer

At the heart of every grievance are fundamental questions about the rights and responsibilities of employment.

Usually when a group approaches an employer with a complaint, they are unhappy with a center-wide decision or with a broad question of the employer's attitude to employees.

Hippity Hop Child Care Center used to be such a nice place to work. But lately things haven't been going so well. Several employees seem to be unhappy. As it turns out, they have different complaints:

Mary took two days off to attend a funeral. When she returned, the director told Mary that the days off would be without pay. There is no funeral leave policy at the center; vacation leave must be requested two weeks in advance. Mary thinks the policy is unfair since she had earned several vacation days.

Anne, an aide at the center, has a new lead teacher who has been critical of her work. Recently, the lead teacher told Anne that they will no longer meet together to plan. From now on, the lead teacher will plan and conduct all teaching activities. Anne will be responsible for clean up after activities and supervision of the children during meals, naptime, and bathroom breaks. Anne has always

been treated as an equal by other lead teachers and resents this new definition of duties.

Lynne, Karen, and Jackie are teachers in the toddler group. They are feeling a growing resentment toward the teachers in the preschool group. From their perspective, the preschool room is consistently given more supplies and equipment than the toddler room.

Why a grievance procedure is necessary

Hippity Hop may sound like a director's nightmare. But keep in mind, it's a nightmare for the employees, too. At the heart of every grievance are fundamental questions about the rights and responsibilities of employment:

- Does an employee have a right to question the decision or actions of the employer?

- Are there some decisions an employee is automatically entitled to question and others that an employee can question only if the employer grants permission?

- If a grievance is of a very serious nature, should an employee be given an opportunity to communicate directly with the owner or board of directors rather than through the normal chain of command?

- If an employee has a right to express a grievance, how can the employee be given a "fair" hearing and protected from being punished for exercising that "right"?

Most employers recognize there are times when an employee's grievance needs to be heard. It may be that a decision affects the employee negatively and the employer is not aware of the full implication of the decision. It may be that an individual supervisor is acting contrary to the intention of the organization. Yet, how does an employer acknowledge these potential failings of the organization and give the employee a chance to petition for a change? The employer must make an enlightened decision, one that spells out the rights of an employee to air a grievance and which set limits on the kinds of grievances and the extent to which a grievance will be heard. These issues should be clearly spelled out in the center personnel policies in a section entitled "Grievance Procedure."

What is a grievance procedure?

A grievance procedure is simply a written statement informing employees that they have a right to express complaints and a right to expect the employer to review and respond to the complaint. The grievance procedure is generally designed to address two basic issues:

1. Interpretation of personnel policy. No matter how clear the personnel policies, there are always judgment call situations, as well as new situations which do not seem to fit the written policies. Because these possibilities exist, the grievance procedure usually allows an employee to seek interpretation or review of personnel policies when necessary. In some grievance procedures, the language is more open-ended, allowing the employee to question other kinds of center decisions which have a clear relationship to the employee's specific job.

2. Employee-supervisor conflict. Incidents of sharp disagreement between an individual employee and the immediate supervisor occur in early care and education as in all work settings. A grievance procedure accepts that reality and explains how an employee can appeal a decision or action of the supervisor to a level of supervision higher in the organization. If there is no clear way to express a grievance, there is a danger that a weak supervisor becomes a petty dictator and the director or owner will not be aware of the problem.

Acknowledging the employee's right to file a grievance also implies an

---

The Supervisory Process

Employees at the Hippity Hop Center can expect consistent, direct, and constructive information from their supervisor about their work. Supervisors are responsible for helping staff develop the skills and abilities necessary to function successfully in their positions.

After completing the probationary period, employees are assumed to possess the basic skills and qualities necessary for their position. The goal of supervision for these employees is to assure that these skills and qualities are reflected in day-to-day activities, to promote personal and professional growth, and to insure that the center's policies and program philosophy are effectively carried out.

The basic elements in the supervisory process include:

• A clear statement of what is expected through job descriptions and written center policies.

• An opportunity to participate in establishing individual goals.

• A regular mechanism for reviewing information about job performance, including regular meetings with the supervisor or an annual written employee evaluation.

---

employee responsibility. The employee should use every means possible to resolve the conflict directly with the supervisor before resorting to the center's grievance mechanism. In some personnel policies, the employer includes a description of the purpose and process of supervision as a way of emphasizing how disagreements should be resolved routinely.

For a sample grievance procedure and statement of supervisory policy, see "College Avenue School Grievance Procedure" (next page) and "The Supervisory Process" (above).

What should be included?

The grievance procedure is basically the description of a process: It should state who can initiate a grievance. Most centers allow any employee to initiate a grievance, although some

centers limit this right to full time employees (as opposed to part time or probationary employees). Some centers allow the employee to file the grievance verbally but most require a written statement before the grievance can be formally reviewed. Describing who should receive the grievance is important, especially in larger early care and education organizations. Should it be the educational coordinator, director, owner, board of directors, or who?

The next issue is how the complaint will be reviewed. Usually a hearing is held within a specified number of days. The employee is allowed to present the grievance fully. In supervisory disputes, the supervisor is also present and is given equal opportunity to explain the situation. Some grievance procedures stipulate that only the employee is allowed to be present at the hearing, while others allow the employee to have witnesses (for the purpose of presenting information) or an advisor present.

In some policies, the employee is responsible for proposing a "remedy." That is, the employee must describe the change or action which needs to occur in order for the grievance to be resolved.

The procedure should also assure prompt employer action by stating when a decision on the grievance will be made. Usually the hearing is held within one or two weeks after the grievance is filed, and a final decision about the grievance is made as soon after the hearing as possible.

Finally, the grievance procedure may offer a means of appeal. For example, in some centers the director is expected to make a determination on all grievance issues. If the employee is not satisfied with the director's decision, the employee may then appeal to the board of directors (or owner).

Handling a group grievance

If a grievance is filed, it will most likely arise from the interpretation of personnel policy or a supervisory dispute. But what about the example of Hippity Hop where a group of teachers have a grievance? Hopefully, these circumstances will never occur at your center, but you do need to think about how to handle such a grievance.

Usually when a group approaches an employer with a complaint, they are unhappy with a center-wide decision or with a broad question of the employer's attitude towards employees. There are lots of possible examples. The issue could be salaries, staff scheduling, a decision to open or close a particular classroom or program, or favoritism of one group of staff over another by the director.

College Avenue School Grievance Procedure

Initiation of Grievance

- Any permanent employee or group of employees (group may include probationary employees).

- Any parent or group of parents with a child or children presently enrolled in the school.

- Any employee or group of employees of College Avenue Baptist Church.

The complaint must be submitted in written form and signed by all complainants. It must be specific and with documentation of complaint or grievance and with a list of steps already taken to solve the problem.

To Whom Complaint is Addressed

- The initial grievance must be presented to the director in writing. A reasonable time for solution of a grievance must be agreed upon by the director and complainants. A third and neutral party may be called upon to negotiate this time line.

- If no resolution is forthcoming, the grievance may be taken to:
  — the Minister of Education of College Avenue Baptist Church and/or
  — the Children's Committee of the Christian Education Council of College Avenue Baptist Church.

Either of these parties must respond in writing to the complainants within one working week with an outline of their planned course of action. This may include follow-up study, conference with director, or a specific action.

Follow Up

- The written grievance must be responded to with a written proposal for solution and within a period of 15 working days.

- All staff involved in this procedure are guaranteed no undue retaliatory action.

Grievances That Apply to This Procedure

The following are complaints that are valid grievances:

- Breach of licensing regulations.

- Detriment of health and safety of children and/or staff.

- Breach of fair labor standards.

Reprinted from Staff Handbook of the College Avenue School in San Diego, California — Kathryn Prickett, director.

Often when grievance procedures are established, the owner or board does not envision using them to cover a group situation. Although the interpersonal dynamics of a group grievance are complex, the principles for handling the grievance are similar to any other individual grievance and can be used to give the group a fair and objective hearing.

Some centers address the issue of group grievances in personnel policies, although not necessarily directly. These centers include statements which talk about communication, decisionmaking, or even conflict resolution. For example, they might describe the purpose of staff meetings, how often staff meetings are held, and what role staff is expected to play. They might also discuss how staff are involved in making certain kinds of program decisions related to curriculum, equipment, or other decisions affecting daily work or the long term success of the center. These statements show staff that they will be listened to. They describe the appropriate time and place to raise questions or state disagreements. The more these mechanisms are provided, the less likely that the center will be caught by surprise some day with a group grievance.

Is Your Salary Schedule Up to Speed?

by Roger Neugebauer

Low pay has been a hot topic for many years in the early childhood arena — and deservedly so. There is no question that people employed in our profession are seriously underpaid. If more resources were available for salaries, this would relieve a great deal of stress from employees and centers, and environments for children would improve.

But even within a strictly limited budget, there is much a center can do to improve center performance by the way it structures its salary schedule. In this article, I will offer some ideas on how to evaluate the impact of your salary schedule.

This article is the result of an analysis of more than 100 salary schedules submitted by Exchange Panel of 200 members. Based on this review, here are four basic questions to consider in evaluating your current salary schedule:

1.
What are we paying for?

Sometimes it's important to step back and ask some really basic questions: *Why are we paying people? What are we expecting to get in return?*

In early childhood centers, when you hire someone, you could be . . .

- paying for time;
- paying for skills; or
- paying for results.

You need to decide which of these factors you are paying for, because your choice dramatically impacts how you pay people.

If you are paying for time, your assumption is that you are paying for a warm body to fulfill ratio requirements over a period of time. In order to maintain adequate coverage, you would simply need to pay enough to attract and retain staff who meet minimum legal requirements.

If you are paying for skills, your assumption is that people knowledgeable and practiced in early childhood education will perform significantly better than persons without training and experience. Therefore, you would tailor your salary schedule to attract well prepared individuals and to reward their continuing acquisition of knowledge and skills.

If you are paying for results, your assumption is that all that really matters is who performs well on the job. You would design your salary schedule to reward those who are effective performers.

It is my observation that large numbers of centers behave as if they are simply paying for time. By not attaching any monetary value to skills or performance, these centers get what they pay for — mediocre to poor performance.

On the other hand, the overwhelming majority of salary schedules I reviewed for this article reflect a strong bias toward paying for knowledge and skills. There is considerable research support for this bias. The landmark 1976 National Day Care Study concluded that ". . . caregivers with education/training relevant to young children deliver better care with somewhat superior developmental effects for children (Ruopp)." More current research, the 1988 National Child Care Staffing Study, found that teachers with either a bachelor's degree or specialized training in early childhood education at the college level exhibited higher quality caregiving (Whitebook).

Less than 5% of the salary schedules reviewed gave significant weight to on-the-job performance in setting salary levels. Many centers require that employees receive a satisfactory rating before receiving a step increase, but very few awarded significant upgrades for above average performance.

2.
Is our pay equitable?

The premise behind the equity issue is that people should receive equal pay for equal work. There are several ways to evaluate equality of pay — you can compare the pay of a teacher in your center with the pay of people doing comparable work in other professions, teachers in other centers, or other teachers within your own center.

Clearly the pay of early childhood teachers compares poorly to the pay of kindergarten teachers, for example. Many centers are struggling creatively to take small steps toward narrowing this gap. Only a concerted effort by a broad spectrum of players in the early childhood arena will make a serious impact.

Equity from center to center is another matter altogether. A center committed to providing quality services certainly wants to attract and retain the best teachers available. One way to do this is to offer salaries above the community average. At least once every two years, you should do a market survey on teacher salaries in your community to make sure you are not falling behind. In addition, you should keep an eye on salaries offered by new centers when they open.

It is also important to be alert to equity issues within your own center. Sometimes when you have a mix of new and long-term teachers, inequities will develop. You may pay two teachers performing the same job with the same level of performance at significantly different levels. This can potentially be discouraging to the lower paid teacher.

3.
Should we offer annual increases?

Centers grant salary increases based on the following factors:

- responsibility;
- longevity;
- cost of living; and
- performance.

It is possible that there still exist a few staff cooperatives where all staff members are paid the same regardless of the job they perform. With these possible exceptions, all centers today offer increased salaries as staff assume new jobs with increasing responsibility within the center.

Most centers also make some provision for granting annual increases based on longevity and/or cost of living. While such increases are viewed as important and expected, the way in which they are administered does raise some interesting questions and consequences.

Longevity salary increases are based on the assumption that the longer persons work in a job, the better they will perform. While this may be true in some professions, there is little evidence to support it in early childhood. The National Day Care Study found little relationship between years of early childhood experience and caregiver or child behaviors (Ruopp). The National Child Care Staffing Study found "child care experience is a poor predictor of

teacher behavior toward children" (Whitebook).

From these findings we draw several conclusions. If we want teachers' performance to improve, we can't abandon them in their classrooms. We need to provide continuous feedback, regular training, and ready support to help them improve. Using longevity as a reason for raising salaries without any reference to improved performance does not appear to be justified.

Cost of living adjustments are made to compensate for the impact of inflation. If an employee's salary stays the same but the cost of living increases, her salary has in effect decreased.

Not all employees are equally impacted by inflation. Someone earning $30,000 per year is not nearly as impacted by a 5% increase in the cost of bread as someone earning $10,000. However, since the average early childhood teacher earns just below the poverty level (Whitebook), there is little question that annual adjustments are of vital importance for most employees in this profession. For a center to guarantee annual cost of living adjustments could be a hollow promise. Every salary increase must be paid for with a commensurate rise in income. If your center gives an across the board cost of living increase of 5% and your income declines 5%, you could be courting disaster. Many centers inject this reality into their personnel policies with statements such as "Every effort will be made to provide annual cost of living raises subject to the availability of funds."

Such cautious promises offer scant assurance to staff members living on the edge of poverty. If the center can't give an annual increase, they will have to wait 12 months for a much needed raise. Certainly being sincere about exploring every avenue to increase salaries is essential.

Another small way to ease anxiety is to review financial projections quarterly or semi-annually with the idea of offering smaller, more frequent adjustments. (Of course, then you will have to figure out a way to alleviate the stress on your bookkeeper.)

Determining the amount of an annual cost of living adjustment is not an exact science. Many companies peg their increases to the Consumer Price Index (CPI). The CPI is calculated by the price of goods and services purchased by a family of four with an annual income of $12,000. This index, therefore, has little relevance for families of different sizes or in higher income brackets. But because the majority of early childhood teachers do earn under $12,000, the CPI is a fairly reliable measure for centers to use as a benchmark.

4.
Should we offer merit raises?

There is much to be said for paying for performance instead of longevity. You want staff who work hard and continue to improve to believe that their contributions are valued. You can show appreciation by frequently observing and acknowledging their good deeds, by providing all the materials and moral support they need, and by publicly praising their performance. However, it is hard to give a clearer, more welcome signal than cash.

Clearly people don't gravitate to early childhood for its financial benefits. Over and over again, teacher surveys have shown that the true rewards of teaching relate to making a difference in the lives of children. However, at some point, even the most committed teacher will become discouraged if year after

year they do a great job for the center but are paid no more than anyone else, or less than teachers in other centers.

If your center is considering granting merit raises, here are some points to consider:

• **Merit raises should not be given in place of cost of living increases, but in addition to them.** If raises are only given to exceptional performers, you run the risk of alienating the majority of your teachers who may be performing adequately but not spectacularly. Some centers employ systems whereby teachers with unsatisfactory performance are not given raises, those with satisfactory performance are given small raises, and those with superior performance are given larger raises.

• **Small merit raises may be more harmful than no raises at all.** Giving an employee a token raise for meritorious performance is more likely to induce cynicism than pride. If you are going to award merit raises, they must be perceived as worthy of the effort.

• **A merit raise system is only as effective as the evaluation system upon which it is based.** If you are going to base pay on performance, you need to be sure you are measuring performance objectively and fairly. You need to have in place an evaluation instrument that all staff view as valid. (Having their input in its development will go a long way toward establishing its validity.) Those performing the evaluations must be skilled at observing and giving feedback.

• **Annual evaluations for salary determination should not be viewed as a substitute for ongoing employee appraisals.** If an employee is to use supervisory feedback to improve her performance, this

feedback needs to be frequent, non-judgmental, and nonthreatening. An annual salary evaluation goes against all of these guidelines. Even with a merit raise evaluation system in place, you need to regularly engage in giving specific, objective feedback to employees to give them the information they need to improve their own performance.

As a center director, you need to invest your limited resources wisely in order to maintain a stable, high quality organization. We recommend, wherever possible, giving a combination of cost of living and merit raises. You need to bring out the best in your staff by rewarding their great efforts as individuals as well as by doing everything in your power to raise the salaries of all teachers.

References and Resources

Ruopp, R., et al. (1979). *Children at the Center*. Cambridge, MA: Abt Associates.

Sibson, R. E. (1990). *Compensation (Fifth Edition)*. New York: AMACOM.

Townsend, R. (1984). *Further Up the Organization*. New York: Alfred A. Knopf.

Viscott, D., MD. (1985). *Taking Care of Business*. New York: William Morrow and Company, Inc.

Whitebook, M. (1989). *Who Cares? Child Care Teachers and the Quality of Care in America*. Oakland, CA: Child Care Employee Project.

Working for Quality Child Care. National Center for the Early Childhood Work Force, 6536 Telegraph Avenue, Suite A-201, Oakland, CA 94609.

Designing a Job Classification and Wage Scale System

by Mary Ann Anthony

As the American economy continues to grow, creating unprecedented low unemployment across the country, early care and education program directors are challenged with recruiting and retaining qualified staff in a shrinking labor market. At the same time, the demand for quality child care has never been higher. In this pressured environment, wage rates are often arbitrary, depending upon how desperate the director is to hire or retain or which staff member yells loudest for an increase. Staff morale and loyalty always suffer in this atmosphere of grab what you can, and turnover increases as staff seek higher wages or fairer treatment elsewhere. So what is the solution?

The answer is to assess the state of your program's current practices and apply rational thought to your job descriptions, wage scale, and salary increment policies to maximize the effectiveness of your salary budget.

What are the characteristics of a good salary plan?

■ Establishes wages in a systematic way that everyone can understand

■ Reflects levels of pay in the community

■ Reflects relative worth of jobs in the center

■ Fair and consistent in treatment of employees

■ Built on classification of jobs that recognizes degree of difficulty and responsibility

■ Recognizes education and experience of employees

Why have a job classification and wage scale system?

Staff retention. When a clear and definitive career ladder is established, staff can see what it will take to advance professionally and what the rewards will be as they do.

Staff motivation. Staff will have clear incentives to improve their professional qualifications.

Fairness. Because a rational and consistent pay scale related to clearly defined qualifications and job responsibilities is made visible to each staff member in a center, the perception of *deals* and favoritism is eliminated. Though it takes a period of time to fully implement, ultimately staff in the center doing the same job with the same qualifications and longevity will receive equitable compensation.

Improved quality of staff. Staff see the benefit of their own professional development in terms of monetary reward and career advancement. Directors can allocate their precious compensation dollars to get the biggest bang for the buck in terms of staff qualifications.

Enhanced ability to analyze compensation issues. Budgeting becomes easier because wage rates are more predictable. The exercise of comparative wage studies is simplified.

Once you accept the value of having a job classification and wage scale system, there are steps to follow to develop one that reflects the reality of your center. As director, the easy way is to go through these steps in splendid isolation and finish the job in a day or two. However, the staff

Proposed Staff Qualifications/Responsibilities/Wage Scales

POSITION AND MINIMUM QUALIFICATIONS	SALARY RANGES			RESPONSIBILITIES
	LOW (Starting)	MID (2½ Years)	HIGH (5 Years)	
Assistant Teacher, Level I • 16 years old, no experience, no course • Full or part time	$7.00/hour	$7.65/hour	$8.25/hour	Staff/child interaction, staff/staff interaction, implementing curriculum
Assistant Teacher, Level II • High School Diploma/GED • OCCS Teacher Certified • CPR Certified • 1 year experience	$8.00/hour	$8.65/hour with additional course	$9.25/hour with 3 courses	Above, plus staff/parent interaction
Teacher, Level I • Assistant Level II plus 1 additional course or • CDA with 1 year experience • Literate	$10.00/hour ($19,500/year)	$10.80/hour ($21,060/year)	$11.60/hour ($22,600/year)	Above, plus lesson plans, health and safety, child assessment, behavior management, classroom environment
Teacher, Level II • CDA with 2 years experience or • Associate with 1 year experience or • BA with 6 months experience (OCCS Lead Teacher or higher)	$10.75/hour ($21,000)	$11.60/hour ($22,600)	$12.45/hour ($24,200)	Above, plus responsible in absence of lead teacher
Lead Teacher • CDA with additional courses toward degree and 3 years experience or • Associate with 3 years experience or • BA with 18 months experience	$12.00/hour ($23,400)	$12.95/hour ($25,252)	$13.90/hour ($27,100)	Above, plus progress reports, parent confences, responsible for overall program planning
Mentor Teacher (ECE Specialist) • BA and 6-10 years experience or • MA and 4-8 years experience (minimum 3 years in one center, internal candidates only)	$14.00/hour ($27,300)	$15.10/hour ($29,445)	$16.25/hour ($31,600)	Above, plus specialized education duties, mentor less experienced staff, provide training
Assistant Director • Same as Mentor Teacher, but OCCS Director I or II qualified	$14.00/hour ($27,300)	$15.10/hour ($29,445)	$16.25/hour ($31,600)	Supervise lead teachers and teachers, assist director with administrative duties, assume responsibilities in director's absence
Program Director (Center Based) • OCCS Director I or II, 3-5 years experience (center specific) • BA in ECE or related field	$16.40/hour ($32,000)	$17.70/hour ($34,515)	$19.00/hour ($37,118)	Overall responsibilities for program leadership, quality, health and safety, fiscal management
Program Director (Family Child Care) • BA in ECE or social work, 3-5 years supervisory experience				
Provider Coordinator • BA in social work or ECE	$12.30/hour ($23,985)	$13.25/hour ($25,838)	$14.25/hour ($27,800)	Coordinate all activities related to assigned family child care providers
Case Manager • BA in social work or related field				Coordinate and manage all activities relating to assigned clients of family child care program
Director of Child Care Services • MA in ECE, administration, social work, or related field or • BA with MA in progress (additional experience may substitute for MA) • 5-7 years progressively responsible experience in child care, human services • 3-5 years supervisory, adminindistration, community organization	$40,000	$47,500	$55,000	Responsible for carrying out agency's mission and for overall operation of all assigned programs, provide leadership and vision to all program staff

will accept the plan more readily if the process is participatory. A representative committee of staff members will lend credibility and a sense of openness to the project.

Steps to getting started

Do a task analysis and identify the positions and classifications your program needs. This should be done as objectively as possible, without regard for the personalities currently in any of the positions.

Develop job descriptions. These should summarize the information gathered in the task analysis and should consider the following factors:

— Nature of the work itself
— Degree of responsibility
— Responsibility of supervision of others
— Nature of supervision received
— Degree of contact with the public
— Knowledge, skill, or ability required
— Training and experience required

Set minimum qualifications for each position.
— Education
— Experience
— State certification

Classify each position in relation to the others. Develop your ideal functional organizational model and develop a chart which displays your classifications visually.

Survey competitive wages in your community. Consider the relative value of your benefit options when comparing your wages to others.

Establish a wage range for each identified job classification. This is often best expressed as *Low – Mid – High*. Chart this on your classification grid.

Analyze your current employees. Make a list showing their educational level, experience, certification, and current rate of pay. At this point (to protect confidentiality), you will not include your committee.

Determine where your employees fall on your new job classification grid by virtue of their qualifications, NOT by their current job title.

Analyze whether their current wage falls within or outside the new ranges established for their qualification level.

Adjust the pay range for the classification wherever necessary.

Develop a plan to make any necessary adjustments to individual pay rates to conform to the new scale. This could mean phased in incremental increases for staff who fall significantly below the range and position they're in, or it could mean freezing wages for staff who are compensated above their qualification and responsibility level. All new hires will conform to the system from date of hire.

Develop increment policies, considering the following common reasons for granting increases or exceptions:

— Qualifications
— Merit
— Length of service
— Cost of living
— Available resources

Finally, plan to revisit your wage scale periodically to be sure that it still meets your program's needs.

Once your plan is established, revision should be a simple process. It will take some time and a thoughtful plan to eliminate the inequities in your center. Ultimately it should enhance your ability to recruit and retain qualified people. This article has deliberately not addressed the issue of how to pay for an enhanced wage scale. In my experience, an analysis of the competitive wage market and a rationally worked out job classification and wage scale are important tools to use in approaching parents, boards, and other funders for additional salary dollars.

Resources

The following resources are helpful in developing job descriptions or gaining insights on the subject of fair and equitable wage systems:

Bloom, P. J. (May 1993). "But I'm worth more than that! Implementing a comprehensive compensation system." *Young Children*, 67-72.

Center for the Child Care Workforce. (1998). *Creating better child care jobs: Model work standards for teaching staff in center-based child care.* Washington, DC: Center for the Child Care Workforce.

National Child Care Association. (1992). *Sample job descriptions to assist in complying with the Americans With Disabilities Act of 1990.* Atlanta, GA: National Child Care Association.

Southern Regional Education Board. (1979). *Day care personnel management.* Atlanta, GA: Southern Regional Education Board.

Whitebook, M., & Bellm, D. (1999). *Taking on turnover: An action guide for child care center teachers and directors.* Washington, DC: Center for the Child Care Workforce.

Competitive Wage Analysis

Center _____

Date _____

Competitor Name _____

Location _____

Licensed Capacity _____

Employer Sponsored/Subsidized ___ Yes ___ No

Single Site _____ Multi Site _____

POSITION	WAGE RATE			HOURLY/ SALARY	# EMPLOYEES IN POSITION	BONUS Y/N AVG $	BENEFITS						
	LOW	AVERAGE	HIGH				VACATION	SICK	HOLIDAY	PROF DEV	MEDICAL ($)	DENTAL ($)	OTHER
ASSISTANT TEACHER													
TEACHER													
LEAD TEACHER													
TEAM LEADER													
ASSISTANT DIRECTOR													
DIRECTOR													
COOK													
SUBSTITUTE													
OTHER (define)													

Please provide other information you learn about this center that may be helpful in determining wage scales.

_____

_____

_____

_____

_____

_____

_____

Find, Attract, and Retain Workers With Affordable Benefits

by Mark E. Battersby

How can any early childhood program, for-profit or non-profit, hope to compete with large companies whose compensation and motivation programs have grown so complex that a whole new category of software, incentive compensation management, is required? Many child care center owners and directors have discovered that employee benefits can often eliminate the need for incentive compensation or even time sheets or time cards. Providing benefits, things for employees that, if they purchased them for themselves, would normally be considered personal or family expenses, are well-proven motivators. And, best of all, the cost of providing employee benefits, a special type of fringe benefit, is often tax deductible.

Whether for-profit or non-profit, an early care and education program can usually deduct the cost of providing benefits such as accident and health plans, group term life insurance, adoption assistance, dependent care assistance, and educational assistance. Adding to the value of many of these benefits is the fact that the cost of many of them can often be excluded from the recipient's income.

Surprisingly, survey after survey shows that it is not money alone that attracts new workers and keeps existing employees on the job. It is the benefits. And now, thanks to our unique tax laws, every smart director and owner can not only afford to offer fringe benefits to their workers, they may even be able to benefit themselves.

That's right, our tax laws merely prevent an employer from discriminating in favor of owners, key employees, or other highly-compensated individuals when setting up any benefits plan that is to be tax deductible by the child care business and tax-free to the recipient. Those laws do not say that the key employees and owners cannot also benefit from the same *perks* offered every other employee.

Proceed cautiously

Fringe benefits that are not specifically excluded from employees' income must be included in the employees' taxable income, at their value, as well as subject to the payroll taxes that the employer pays. This is also true when the benefits don't meet the federal

requirements. Some types of benefit plans, for instance, are not permitted to discriminate in favor of highly compensated employees, such as the child care business' director or owner. This is particularly true of not-for-profit or non-profit operations.

If the plan is found by the Internal Revenue Service to discriminate, the value of the benefits will generally be treated as taxable compensation to the highly compensated employee who receives them. Of course, the cost of the benefit to the child care business remains tax deductible even if found to discriminate.

What do they want?

According to the results of one widely-publicized survey (US Chamber of Commerce, Washington, DC), the best perk that any employer can give an employee is one that she wants and that costs you little or nothing. Thus, while stock options and big salaries may be needed to lure higher level employees, the average early childhood program can get some pretty good mileage out of some inexpensive perks. A few common ones that consistently get high marks are:

■ Flex time

■ Company discounts

■ Free food and free beverages

- Casual dress Fridays (or full time)

- Education or personal development training (on or after company time).

Notice that among the perks most often chosen by employees only one, education or personal development, actually costs the employer. That's when our tax rules step in to provide a helping hand.

When education is offered as a fringe benefit by a child care center, the payments received by an employee for tuition, fees, books, supplies, etc., under the employer's educational assistance program may be excluded from the employee's income up to $5,250 per year. Although the courses covered by the plan need not be job related, courses involving sports, games, or hobbies may be covered only if they involve the employee's business or are required as part of a degree program.

And, best of all, the child care business, whether for-profit or non-profit, may claim a full tax deduction for the amounts paid. Drawbacks include the necessity of a formal tuition reimbursement plan and, obviously, sufficient cash flow to fund that program.

The basics

First, small employers such as most early childhood program must:

- Allow employees time off to:
  — vote
  — serve on a jury
  — perform military service

- Comply with all requirements of workers' compensation

- Withhold for FICA and FUTA

- Contribute to state disability programs in states where such programs exist (California, Hawaii, New Jersey, New York, Puerto Rico, and Rhode Island).

Those child care centers do not, obviously, have to offer their employees special or unique benefits.

Benefits from benefits

No matter which specific benefits your employees may be clamoring for or which benefits the competition is offering, you need to assess how those benefits will impact on your child care center or business. If, for example, you offer popular benefits such as generous time-off policies or health insurance, you are going to be able to attract — and keep — more and better employees. But will it be worth the cost?

While each employee has different needs, the recent trend has been pointing toward health insurance as the most important and highly valued benefit for employees. Health insurance is tax-deductible to the employer and tax-free for the employee. What's more, a child care business can frequently purchase it at a lower cost than the employee would ordinarily pay for an individual policy.

Some early care and education programs have discovered that, especially if they employ a lot of part-timers, health benefits may not be that important because the employee is getting health benefits from another source (from another full-time job, through a spouse's employer, or through a parent's health insurance). In that case, a smart owner or director would focus on offering other, less expensive benefits, that would still be considered valuable by employees. Or, you may find that employees would prefer more cash compensation rather than any particular benefit.

Keep in mind, however, that although that cash paid in lieu of fringe benefits remain a legitimate, tax deductible business expense for the child care operation, the employee is required to include the amount in his or her income and pay taxes on it. This illustrates the often-overlooked value of fringe benefits programs offered by employers. In addition to the child care operation's tax deduction for the expense of providing fringe benefits, those benefits are usually tax-free to the recipient.

The cheapest may be the most expensive

Bonuses and awards must, as mentioned, be included in an employee's taxable income. Should the bonus or award be in the form of goods or services, employees must include the fair market value of the goods or services in their income. The same applies to holiday gifts. However, employees who receive turkeys, hams, or other similar items of nominal value from their employers at Christmas or other holidays may exclude the value of the gift from their income.

On a similar note, so-called *de minimis* benefits may be worth little or nothing in the eyes of our lawmakers, but can go a long way toward making an employee happy — without an accompanying bill. Under the rules, employees may exclude from their gross income the value of fringe benefits that qualify as de minimis.

De minimis fringe benefits mean any property or service that is so small in value that accounting for it is unreasonable or administratively impractical. Examples include:

- occasional meal money or local transportation fare

- occasional personal use of an employer's copy machine

- occasional cocktail parties, group meals, or picnics for employees and their guests

- inexpensive birthday or holiday gifts (except cash)

- coffee, doughnuts, and soft drinks

- local telephone calls

- flowers, fruit, books, or other similar items given to employees for special occasions or under special circumstances.

If you do go the retirement benefits route

While 401(k) plans are popular with large corporate employers, they are not the most popular plans for small business owners since they severely limit the amount of money that a business owner can sock away on his own behalf. For those early childhood program owners who are going to the trouble and expense of setting up a pension plan, a money-purchase plan would generally offer more flexibility and the opportunity to defer tax on a much larger nest egg.

In a money-purchase plan, the employer is obligated to contribute each year even if the child care center didn't make a profit (taxable or nontaxable). The contributions are determined by a specific percentage of each employee's compensation and must be made annually. The employer may contribute up to the lesser of (1) 25% of the employee's compensation (up to $205,000 maximum deduction); or (2) $42,000 in 2005. For yourself, you can contribute up to $14,000 to a 401(k)-type plan.

Other, less expensive alternatives include:

■ **Simplified Employee Pensions** (SEPs), is a written arrangement that allows an employer to make contributions toward his own and employees' retirement without becoming involved in more complex retirement plans. The contributions are made to special IRAs (SEP-IRA) set up for each individual qualifying employee.

■ **SIMPLE Plans**. A child care center can adopt a relatively new type of simplified retirement plan, the Savings Incentive Match Plan for Employees (SIMPLE). If you want to establish a SIMPLE, it must be the only retirement plan you have; if you've already established another plan you'd have to terminate it or convert it to a SIMPLE.

The plan (SIMPLE Plan) allows employees to make elective contributions of up to $10,000 in 2005 and usually requires employers to make matching contributions — up to 3% of each employee's pay. Alternately, you can decide to make a blanket contribution of 2% of each participating employee's pay regardless of whether they make any elective contributions. These are the only contributions permitted. You cannot opt to contribute more for older employees, managers, or the business owner.

The bottom line

In putting together a benefits package, you need to weigh a number of factors: what benefits are of high value to employers and employees alike; what benefit the employees prefer; what benefits competing centers are offering; and finally, what benefits your center can afford.

Wouldn't it be ironic in this day and age of escalating costs and increased competition for good, qualified employees, if those benefits that offered the most reward to both the child care business' employees and its owners, turned out to be the ones which cost the least?

Mark E. Battersby is a tax and financial writer, columnist, author, and adviser with offices in the suburban Philadelphia community of Ardmore, Pennsylvania. For more than 25 years, Mr. Battersby's features and columns have appeared in leading trade and professional journals. His topical columns are syndicated to over 65 publications each week. He has authored four books.

Chapter 3

Orienting
and
Training Staff

Right From the Start: Changing Our Approach to Staff Orientation

by Margie Carter

Whenever I watch directors launch a new staff member into a classroom, my heart leaps. I see the feeling of relief and the quiet crossing of fingers, hoping this will turn out to be someone who brings stability and a positive contribution to the quality of the program. Yet, time after time, the relief is short lived and things start unraveling for the director, the new staff person, and the rest of the teachers who are longing for a solid new co-worker.

The search for qualified staff is always time consuming, often tentative, and frequently discouraging. If you are fortunate to have some real choices among job applicants, people with an ECE education or several years experience, consider yourself truly blessed. If you are faced with choosing from a less qualified pool, you are certainly not alone. In either case, once you hire new staff your challenge is to keep them, and then keep them growing into your vision for your program.

Growing and keeping your staff requires simultaneous work on three fronts (even as you work on 20 others):

■ budget development to adequately compensate your staff,

■ working conditions and an organizational climate that reflect your vision,

■ staff development and mentoring systems to support individual growth and overall professionalism.

For the most part, from the assessments teachers give me and what I witness myself, I'd say we are failing in all three of these areas. There are certainly exceptions and some innovations underway, but for the most part, we fail teachers right from the start and continue to reap the consequences.

With our limited resources, budget development is a constant strain requiring painful compromises. But even in better resourced programs such as Head Start and employer-sponsored child care, things are usually lean when it comes to an inspiring organizational climate and/or a meaningful staff development system. There may be regular training or staff meetings, but the emphasis is still shaped by regulations and daily business, rather than a bigger dream of who they hope to become. In most programs there is little evidence of overall self-reflection and an excitement about learning among the staff. Though not on most of our checklists, these are key ingredients to quality, and contributors to staff retention.

Taking a new approach

I'd like to suggest a radical alternative to the typical practice of new staff orientation. If, right from the start, we treat staff with the same caring and learning opportunities that we want them to provide for children, our chances of keeping and growing them into a career will be far greater. This means viewing new staff orientation as significantly different from requiring them to report to work an hour before their shift to fill out paper work and hear the nitty-gritty details of their responsibilities. Instead, all new staff should receive one week of paid orientation without direct responsibility for children so that they can experience our vision in action and begin to practice assuming a role in it.

Strategy:
Begin with your vision, values, and assumptions

Typically, the emphasis in new staff orientation is on the safety and supervision of children. While it is important to communicate to staff that safety is our number one responsibility with children, this message can be part of an initial focus on valuing childhood and respecting children. Orientation should not be limited to lengthy explanations, but include a variety of ways to explore your program's vision, values, and assumptions about children's rights, capabilities, and feelings. Short readings can be offered and discussed along with a relevant, engaging video. (*Children at the Center: Reflective Teachers at Work* is useful for this purpose.) Time can be spent observing in classrooms with the director or a mentor at the new teacher's side to narrate how respect for children looks in action.

This first overview day should also include an introduction to your approach to respecting and collaborating with the children's families. Hopefully, you have some engaging questionnaires for parents to fill out, and these can be reviewed along with documentation of examples of partnerships with parents in your program. A short article that conveys how teachers think about their work with children's families would be useful to discuss here. (The articles "Changing Our Attitudes and Actions in Working With Families" and "Developing Meaningful Relationships With Families" serve this purpose well.) You could also have the teacher try exploring some of the questions offered in my earlier *Exchange* article, "Considering Our Curriculum in Working With Families."

Strategy:
Provide time for further observation, reading, and self assessment

Days two and three of your orientation week can be spent with the teacher doing more observation in the classrooms using specific work-sheets to guide a first hand study of how the environment, curriculum, and interactions reflect a set of values. The new teacher can be given an attractive binder for keeping these observation worksheets and the readings that are offered, along with blank pages for reflective writing. Ask the teacher for daily writing on how he is responding and thinking, questions that are coming up, and specific strengths and areas for growth he self-identifies. This initial reflective writing can serve several purposes: it can set the tone for an ongoing practice, help the teacher and director begin to define an initial professional development plan, and lay the ground work for creating a biographical statement as described below.

During these two days, new teachers should study selected documentation, child journals or portfolios, curriculum project books, and notes from important staff meetings. He or she can meet with team members as well as the director or mentor assigned. Time should be spent focusing on what it means to work as a member of a team, how to participate in collaborative discussions and projects, and ways to work through conflicts with respect.

Strategy:
Practice documentation and gain familiarity with available technology

If your program wants teachers to be regularly observing and gathering documentation of children's activities, then offer an opportunity to practice this before assigning direct responsibility for a group of children. In the room where she or he will be working, help the new teacher focus on one child or activity to write up, photograph, and analyze in collaboration with the director, mentor, or teammate. Offer useful resources as an initial introduction to this process (such as *Family-Friendly Communica-tions, The Power of Observation, Spreading the News*) and point to ones that will be useful for further development (*The Art of Awareness, Windows on Learning*).

This would also be a good time to familiarize the new staff member with the staff work space, and the use and maintenance of any technology you have, such as computers, printers, scanners, cameras, and video and tape recorders. Help her locate where other professional development resources are kept, as well as basic educational supplies for the program, first aid, record keeping, and communication systems.

Ask the teacher to go over reflective writing to date and begin to conceptualize a biographical statement as part of a visual display to be created on the last day of orientation. This gives both the teacher practice and will make his thoughts, values, and background visible to others as he joins your staff.

Strategy:
End, rather than begin, with nitty-gritty details and paper work

Starting with a focus on values, vision, and the children and their families sets the tone for the way you want teachers to view their work. When you delay introducing a bundle of details about job responsibilities and focus on the heart of your job, you create a different organizational climate that parallels how you want the teachers to be with the children. Ending the orientation process with paperwork and daily details is less overwhelming and fits into a larger context for new staff who have watched the center functioning for almost a week.

It's also important to end the orientation process with some inspiration, a summing up, and projection of next steps. Giving the person time to create a visual biography board to be posted, as well as clarity about the upcoming probationary period and next steps for professional development, is a fitting conclusion to the first week of an exciting new job.

Calculate the cost of turnover

If you are feeling that you'd never have the time or budget for this approach, I recommend you take a closer look. Staff turnover takes a big toll on our programs. With each coming and going there is a social-emotional toll on the children and adults involved, as well as a time and financial drain on the administration. Turnover costs can run from several hundred dollars per employee to as high as 1.5 times an employee's annual salary according to the valuable resource, *Taking on Turnover*. You probably know this in your bones, but if you find yourself skeptical or unable to convince others, consult this book for its strategies to calculate the costs of turnover in your program. *Taking on Turnover* also includes other valuable guidelines for looking at your work environment, improving compensation, and substitute policies.

Turnover is rarely the result of teachers not understanding all the regulations and requirements of the job. Quite the opposite. We often lose potentially great members of our staff, not only because of inadequate wages, but because we throw them into a deep, olympic-sized pool without giving them carefully fitted goggles and a clear life support system. How can they become long distance swimmers if our orientation and ongoing staff development is only focused on treading water?

Perhaps the idea of keeping a new teacher out of the classroom for a week's orientation leaves you gasping for air as you consider patching together coverage with no substitutes or slack in your budget. But if you want new teachers to make a long term investment in your program, you have to begin with a significant investment in them. If you offer this time and respect to them, they are more likely to offer it to the children and families in your program.

Resources

Curtis, D., & Carter, M. (2000). *The Art of Awareness: How Observation Can Transform Your Teaching.* St. Paul, MN: Redleaf Press.

Carter, M., & Curtis, D. (1996). *Spreading the News.* St. Paul, MN: Redleaf Press.

Carter, M., & Curtis, D. (1997). *Children at the Center: Reflective Teachers at Work.* Seattle, WA: Harvest Resources.

Carter, M. (July, 2000). "Considering Our Curriculum in Working With Families." *Exchange, 134*(90-93).

Carter, M. (November, 1999). "Developing Meaningful Relationships With Families." *Exchange, 130*(63-65).

Diffily, D., & Morrison, K. (Eds). (1996). *Family-Friendly Communications for Early Childhood Programs.* Washington, DC: NAEYC.

Helm, J. H., Beneke, S., & Steinheimer, K. (1998). *Windows on Learning.* New York: Teachers College Press.

Hilliard, D., & Pelo, A. (March, 2001). "Changing Our Attitudes and Actions in Working With Families." *Exchange, 138*(48-51).

Jablon, J. R., Dombro, A. L., & Dichtelmiller, M. L. (1999). *The Power of Observation.* Washington, DC: Teaching Strategies, Inc.

Whitebook, M., & Bellm, D. (1999). *Taking on Turnover.* Washington, DC: Center for the Child Care Workforce.

Margie Carter is a college instructor, author, and speaker who travels widely to work with early childhood programs. She thanks teacher Ann Pelo for the thoughts she contributed to this article.

Motivating Adults to Learn

by Karen Miller

"I pay for them to go to all kinds of training, but getting them to implement what they've learned is a real challenge."

One of our e-mail network members expressed difficulty in motivating some experienced infant teachers to keep on learning. They were resistant to new ideas and the concept of *curriculum* for infants, in spite of several meetings and the advice of consultants. Of course, this is not an isolated situation. It doesn't matter if the new idea is a handwashing technique, a way to interact with parents, a method for observing and recording, or curriculum practices, staff sometimes resist change. Our network members shared many ideas for making learning a *norm* in your program.

Causes of resistance

Understanding the basis of the reluctance to learn new things helps us think of ways to overcome it.

■ **Failure to see the need**. Many centers and state regulations require ongoing education. Linda Gillespie says staff may wonder why they need to learn something and how it applies to their work and life. When we can't make that connection, it's hard to motivate others. Adult learners have to feel it's worth their while. This is where you can talk about research studies, show them other programs, or have people experienced in the method talk to them. Lynn Manfredi/Petitt speculates that their thinking may be linked to the idea that mothers (supposedly) know intuitively what to do with their children. *"They* don't get trained, so why should we?" Of course, something that works perfectly well with one or two children may simply not be reasonable in a group setting. It is the job of the trainer to point that out. The first message of training is to communicate how children will benefit from the practice or why it is necessary.

■ **Risk of Failure or of Judgment**. There might be genuine doubt that the new concept will *work*, or the person may fear they may not be able to *pull it off*. It helps to set things up in an experimental mode. "Next time *A* happens, try *X*. If that doesn't help, we can go back to the drawing board." "Try it for a week," is another good suggestion. Then, be there to support the person's efforts and encourage them. "You might try . . . ," is another good phrase, or "Here is what some other people have done that worked well . . . " Most importantly, let them know you don't expect perfection right away.

■ **Guilt**. A person may feel criticized for doing something *the wrong way* for so long. Lynn Manfredi/Petitt shares this story: "One co-worker finally admitted to me that she was concerned that she had done it *wrong* with her children — who were at that moment challenging teens. We have to get our own fears and insecurities out of the way in order to learn new things."

■ **Time/Money**. Peggy Yackel states, "One of the problems in our profession is that it pays so poorly that many of our unmarried staff have to work at evening and week-end jobs to make ends meet so they have little energy to grow professionally." Naturally, offering as much time and support during working hours is helpful.

■ **Feeling Overwhelmed**. Mike Casey suggests, do a little bit at a time. It can be overwhelming to think you have to totally change the way you've been working for a number of years. Break the topic down. If it's an outside workshop over a broad topic, help them identify a piece of it to work on first.

Strategies

- Locate quality conferences in your area that have an infant track and request that the staff attend. Hearing what other centers are doing, especially if it is innovative, usually motivates staff. They develop a sense of collegiality and realize they are not the only ones asked to practice in a certain way. They can gain insights and conviction.

- It's great if you can close your program and send the entire staff to conferences. This is one way of supporting them with time and money and shows you value them. Plus, the break from their ordinary routine can give people new energy.

- Put one staff person in charge of keeping track of in-service training. Peggy Yackel does this for her program and is forever bringing in announcements of classes, conferences, and reading — urging others to take advantage of them.

- Ask staff for input as to what kind of training they'd like brought in to the center.

- Arrange a visit to another center, perhaps where people could see others using a new method or implementing interesting ideas.

- Provide articles from professional magazines for people to read. One director has subscriptions to many early childhood professional publications. She glances through them and notes the pertinent articles. Then, she attaches a note on the cover listing good articles to read and puts them in staff mailboxes with a note to read, initial, and pass on.

- Provide staff with the newest books on infant and toddler care.

- Use teaching videos and view them. Arrange for everyone to view the video separately or call a staff meeting and have everyone view it at once and discuss it.

- Identify one or two staff who may be the least resistant and ask them to do a little research/reading on the issue. They will help the others to understand what you are trying to do.

- Build on what is known and commonly done by the group and use long-time teachers as class mentors. Ask people to share ideas and questions in writing on group charts. This helps people feel valued and *heard*.

- Encourage membership in a professional association. Suggest to parents of ECE students to give them the membership as a gift. Or you might provide this membership to teachers who have *proved* themselves.

- Hold a team building workshop at your center. It is a good way to ensure that new people on staff feel supported and included.

- Appeal to staff self-interest. Show them how the new practice will make their jobs easier or more effective.

Coming to "Ah-ha"

As a trainer, I can share that it is a delightful experience when you sense that people are *getting it* in a presentation. You can see the *light bulbs* go on over their heads. There is usually a sense of excitement and eagerness to apply new understandings. You hear people say things like, "I can't wait to get back to my children and try this." In order to reach this point, you must get people past the *Yes-buts*. Some people resist change, perhaps because of defensiveness. They might understand the principles of what you are saying and agree with you, but fear a lack of support from their administration or co-workers.

Back at the center, make sure staff are supported in their growth. Be a cheerleader. Ask them what they need from you. Notice their efforts and express appreciation for successes. Help them notice the change in the children as well.

Motivation comes from within

Cathy Jo Banas points out that you really can't *motivate* someone. Motivation has to come from the heart and a sincere desire to bond with children and do what's best for them. You can, however, facilitate and encourage others.

I have found an irony in training people — the ones who need it the most don't show up or are the most resistant! It's the *old pros* who are already wonderful teachers, who are the most eager learners. Peggy Yackel is quick to point out that age is not a determiner. In fact, it is often older staff who have the perspective and flexibility to be the best learners. The ones who are less interested in trying new teaching methods, she says, are often less educated or have previously taught in a completely different type of program and are reluctant to take all the time required outside the classroom to read.

Don't give up. When people are offered good learning experiences, they feel supported and valued. Everyone, especially those who work with young children, should keep stretching — physically and mentally! It gives vitality to their program and to their lives. Human development never stops.

Karen Miller is the author of (among other titles) **Simple Steps: Developmental Activities for Infants, Toddlers and Twos** *and the newly revised version of* **Things to Do With Toddlers and Twos.**

Thanks to the following members of our e-mail network who contributed significantly to this article: Cathy Jo Banas, lead infant teacher at Intergenerational Learning Center in Apple Valley, MN; Mike Casey, owner and executive director of Shrewsbury Children's Center in Shrewsbury, MA; Annie Diehl, director of the KidsUnlimited Children's Center in Riverside, CA; Linda Gillespie, of the Early Care and Education Resource Development Department of the Community Coordinated Child Care of Union County, NJ; Lynn Manfredi/Petitt, consultant and infant/toddler specialist in the Atlanta area; Phyllis Porter, lead infant teacher and staff trainer at Mount Olivet Day Services in Bloomington, MN; and Peggy Yackel, lead infant teacher at the Westwood Early Childhood Center in St. Louis Park, MN.

Insights into Developing the Emergent Teacher

by Patricia Scallan Berl

The early childhood workforce is changing. More than ever before, directors must contend with faculty whose educational levels, job expectations, and career aspirations differ widely. Teachers vary in their experience, professional demeanor, stages in career development, and most recently, generational differences that impact the significance and commitment work holds for them. Today, directors can no longer look to a single solution when designing staff development. Instead, they must apply both insight and strategy to create effective training programs that meet the needs of a diverse faculty. They need an approach that not only addresses job knowledge and skills, but also recognizes the impact of career life cycle on teachers' goals, attitudes, and motivation.

The beginning teacher's plight

While each teacher is unique in her knowledge, skills, and motivation, the needs and concerns of new teachers are especially crucial and often times challenging. Beginning teachers come fresh to teaching. While they are eager and imaginative, they can also be impatient, opinionated, and very passionate about their beliefs. High on ideals but low in self-confidence, beginning teachers want to do well and to be good teachers.

For a new teacher, the transition from being a student or an associate teacher to lead teacher can be daunting. There are classroom environments to be organized, team roles and responsibilities to be learned, regulatory systems to follow, an organizational culture to understand, and many policies and procedures to correctly implement.

The self-esteem of the novice teacher is fragile and easily influenced by the center's culture and work climate. The well intended remarks of colleagues may be viewed as encouraging or critical. Parents can come across as constantly observing and evaluating the new teacher's classroom practices. Even worse, senior teachers may appear distant, disinterested, or unengaged, further contributing to a beginning teacher's sense of isolation and loneliness.

Whether beginning teachers' self-esteem, attitudes, and competencies are defined by their successes in the classroom and their relationships with colleagues and parents, or by their failures and frustrations in teaching, they exert a profound influence upon the mental health of the children in our care. So, the degree to which a teacher is confident or fearful, kind or hostile, helpful or uncaring, matters greatly for the teacher and the children in her care (Brower, 1973).

What beginning teachers want

A number of years ago, the National Institute of Mental Health (NIMH) engaged first and second year teachers in a series of discussions about their work, how they felt about their first year of teaching, their interactions with parents and colleagues, their personal goals and successes, and the obstacles they encountered along the way. A significant finding of this study was the degree to which new teachers were unable to define their own emotional rewards from teaching. Some had grown so discouraged or become so exhausted that they ceased individual effort or innovative thinking. They tried to be as self sufficient and competent as possible while following the lines of least resistance and least anxiety. In the words of one teacher:

I've considered leaving teaching. I began by saying teaching is marvelous — I've never done anything so fantastic in my life, and I really feel that way. But by the end of the year, I was so unhappy with everything; I considered maybe I should leave. You know it really isn't just one day, though one bad day can make many days miserable. It's not the kids; it's not the adults, either. But there are days when I really would like someone to come to my room, watch me, and say, "Oh marvelous, I've never seen a better teacher." You know, maybe once every two weeks someone could do that for me it would make my two weeks. It's silly I suppose but I guess I need approval from other people.
— Brower, 1973

Additional research on teacher motivation, representing over 600 first year teachers in New York City, revealed that 92% of beginning teachers did not seek help directly from colleagues. They admitted being afraid of acknowledging uncertainty or problems in their classrooms. At best new teachers swapped stories about problems informally and attempted to hide weaknesses from colleagues (ASCD, 1986). The study identified the following needs of the new teacher:

24% moral support and feedback
20% help in classroom management and guidance
18% assistance in lesson plans and curriculum
15% assistance in managing transitions and routines
6% help motivating other staff
2% help in individualizing program for students

In this same study, experienced mentor teachers were polled and

identified new teachers as needing help with curriculum, classroom management, child transitions, and individualizing curriculum.

Cultivating a disposition for development

Elizabeth Jones has addressed the challenge of training emerging teachers in her book *Growing Teachers: Partnerships in Staff Development*. She applies the construct of "growing" versus "training" when working with new teachers. Jones believes the term "training" suggests a kind of rigidity or shaping of development toward a specific end, whereas growth implies a developmental process that nurtures the unique potential within each individual. She writes:

Growing teachers is different from training them. Like emergent curriculum, emergent teacher development is open ended, where philosophy and practice are defined but outcomes are teacher directed, where teachers participate actively in the construction of knowledge about their work, making choices among options for their personal growth. Teachers participate actively in the construction of knowledge about their work, making choices among options for growth.
— Jones, 1993

An effective supervisor of beginning teachers is someone who acts as a facilitator or coach, rather than as an evaluator who is prescriptive or critical of teaching practices. In the mentoring role, the senior teacher is an observant coach, describing what is happening during classroom interactions, encouraging the new teacher to be self-reflective through strategically considered questions such as, "What has just happened?" "What do you think might be happening?" "What did you notice?" and "Why?".

By phrasing the dialogue in this way, the beginning teacher is encouraged

to learn about teaching by practicing the teaching script, observing what happens, and discussing all the possibilities within her repertoire of skills and those of others around her. It is through this interplay of active learning and reflection that emerging teachers come to see themselves as professionals who are capable of making appropriate choices for their children and for themselves, thereby reinforcing their competency and motivation to teach.

Jones notes that coaching alone is not always sufficient to address the needs of emerging teachers. There are baseline competencies required of all staff to meet basic program standards. These are the non-negotiables that are determined by licensing agencies, NAEYC accreditation, and program policies that are set by organizations and enforced by administrators and supervisors.

In many situations, especially within the regulatory environment, the letter of the law applies. Compliance, not creativity, is the desired outcome and all classrooms or teachers are expected to be alike in their adherence to certain established criteria in the realm of health and safety procedures, child guidance, and sometimes, prescribed curriculum. Jones remarks that just as there are times when we offer children many opportunities to make decisions for themselves, and times when we must act on their own behalf and limit choices or direct their behavior, there are times when comparable rules must be learned and standards to be met, for responsible teaching to occur (Jones, 1993).

Applying adult development theory

Over the past three decades, studies in adult maturation, stages of life span, and transitions have been the impetus for new views on training

Principles for Working With Emergent Teachers

■ Focus discussions on teachers' understandings of situations — their ideas, concepts, assumptions about how children learn, what works and doesn't, what they expect of themselves, what others expect of them, their roles and responsibilities.

■ Strengthen opportunities for developing desirable dispositions, focusing on behaviors that are complimentary to effective teaching, such as openness to children's ideas and feelings, inventiveness, resourcefulness, patience, and enthusiasm.

■ Along with the attention to acquiring new skills, also provide opportunities to practice and refine already existing skills, that enable new teachers to apply developing competencies in a more reliable, consistent, or confident manner.

■ Build upon long-term relationships with emerging teachers and curtail one's own eagerness to be helpful or to intervene in an effort to establish one's own credibility or expertise.

■ When a change in an approach or behavior is needed, try phrasing your suggestions in an experimental or nonjudgmental form, such as, "Next time X comes up . . . you could try Y" and see if it helps.

■ Cultivate a habit of suspending judgment by not making corrections too quickly. There is the risk of losing future opportunities to help beginning teachers by alienating them early on, by premature or hastily given corrections.

■ Avoid the temptation to judge the rightness or goodness of what we see, or to assess whether the teacher is doing things *my way* or not. Rather ask, "Why is the teacher responding to the situation in this way?" or "Why is this happening?". In seeking answers to questions, rather than judging events, mentors are much more likely to learn those things that will increase their capacity to help a teacher. (Katz, 1993)

■ Provide new teachers with many choices among a variety of resources to build empowerment and independence.

and development (Bloom, Sheerer, & Britz, 1991). Building on the work of Erickson (1968), Levine (1989), and Sheehy (1995), stages of adulthood or life cycle theory view an individual's development as a continuous process that occurs in sequential stages. Stages are characterized by degrees of equilibrium, disequilibrium, and resolution. At each stage, our attitudes, what motivates us, our self-esteem, competency and flexibility in adapting to change are affected. Our

progression, stagnation, or regression through each stage profoundly impacts our life, work, and relationships.

Lilian Katz has applied the stages of adult life cycle to identify sequential stages in teachers' professional growth patterns. In Katz's model, beginning teachers are in the survival stage, where their main concern is coping and learning the rules. Overwhelmed by all the new tasks and

responsibilities, the new teachers lack confidence, and their feelings are dominated by self-doubt and a strong need for acceptance (Bloom, Sheerer, & Britz, 1991).

In the survival stage, the individual's main psychological task is the search for identity, autonomy, and independence. This stage is characterized by constant disequilibrium and tension, where the individual may struggle as he or she attempts to assert himself or herself as an adult, at work and at home. Emergent teachers in the survival stage may still be living at home, dependent upon parents or family for many things, yet wanting to be seen and treated as adults. They may be exploring intimate relationships or commitment for the first time. They are also reaching beyond home and families, to create their own social community. In applying Katz's model to emerging teachers in the survival stage, supervisors and mentors need to provide teachers with:

■ clear definitions of what is expected
■ help with technical and organizational skills
■ measurable goals they can achieve
■ recognition of successes and positive outcomes
■ opportunities for independent thinking and self reflection
■ guidance in supervising others
■ help with prioritizing tasks, goals, and outcomes
■ detailed discussions on center policy and procedures

To work most effectively with a beginner teacher, the trainer or mentor ideally possesses the following characteristics:

■ acts as a facilitator or trainer, rather than a supervisor
■ is nonjudgmental
■ is not overly friendly, respects personal boundaries, and does not fall into the *"mom"* trap

- recognizes that volatility characterizes many relationships at this stage
- appreciates the needs of new teachers to socialize at work
- helps beginning teachers anticipate and avoid crisis modes
- counsels the unsuccessful teacher out of teaching when it is clear that he or she is not well suited to teaching

For teachers in the survival stage focus staff training on hands-on activities, direct coaching, guided observation, workshops on survival skills, articles, videos, journal writing, discussion groups, and computer-based training that pinpoints specific areas for development.

A word on encouragement and praise

Many emerging teachers cope admirably with the complex tasks and responsibilities they face. They may not need the newest technique, curriculum book, or piece of advice we are dying to share with them. They may simply need a moment of acknowledgement, a word of encouragement, or a note of appreciation that renews and sustains their efforts, helping to instill in them enough enthusiasm and self esteem to keep working in a challenging, unglamorous, and often underappreciated job.

It is important that inspirational messages be specifically related to the work setting and its characteristics, rather than be a generalized message of good will (Katz, 1973). Supportive and encouraging messages work best when they contain real and useful information about the significance of the teacher's efforts. For instance, be specific and say, "Those new science activities

intrigued the children today" rather than "The science activity was great." In giving praise, a supervisor or mentor of emergent teachers should be warm, encouraging, and supportive, yet not excessively close, since this can inhibit one's ability to evaluate progress realistically or perceive and confront serious weaknesses.

Final thoughts on the emergent teacher

Training becomes a means by which new teachers acquire role definition, teaching style, teaching techniques, and professional identification (Katz, 1974). Because developing teachers is more the practice of art than science, a *"one-size fits all approach"* can no longer be the template for today's programs. Rather, training that incorporates a developmental perspective can powerfully influence teacher competency, motivation, and career life cycle. It is the interplay of these factors that becomes the catalyst for shaping training content, its methodology and the long term learning outcomes for teachers. In the words of Lilian Katz:

Each individual brings about his and her own unique challenges. Every teacher we work with has an inner life of concerns, dreams, wishes, fantasies, hopes and aspirations. While we may not always know the content of that life, if we respect the fact that it is there, we are more likely to treat the teacher with dignity and with respect, an approach not only essential in teaching but also ethically sound.
— Katz, 1973

Sources

Association for Supervision and Curriculum Development. Annual Conference in Los Angeles, 1985.

Bloom, P. J., Sheerer, M., & Britz, J. (1991). *Blueprint for Action*. Mt. Rainier, MD: Gryphon House.

Bower, E. M. (1973). *Teachers Talk About Their Feelings*. National Institute of Mental Health, Center for Studies of Child and Family Mental Health.

Jones, E. (1993). *Growing Teachers: Partnerships in Staff Development*. Washington, DC: NAEYC.

Katz, L. G. (October, 1993). "Helping Others with Their Teaching." ERIC Clearinghouse.

Katz, L. G. (1974). "Issues and Problems in Teacher Education." Teacher Education, of the Teacher, by the Teacher, for the Child. Publication of NAEYC conference proceedings.

Katz, L. G. (1991). National Association for the Education of Young Children. Presentation at the Annual Conference.

Sheehy, G. (1995). *New Passages, Mapping Your Life Across Time*. New York: Random House.

Patricia Scallan Berl is a division vice president of mid-Atlantic operations for Bright Horizons Family Solutions. She is known nationally as a conference presenter and author of articles in child care center management and supervision. She has been a regular contributor to Exchange since 1978. In addition to her lovely family, Patricia has a passion for orchids, Springer Spaniels, and travel.

Tolerance or Transformation: What's Our Training Goal?

by Margie Carter

Attending conferences around the country over the last few years, I've noticed that the offering of anti-bias workshops has dwindled. Conference planners tell me that there is no longer much excitement about the topic and the few workshops offered on anti-bias topics are not well attended. I find myself both puzzled and disturbed about this, yet not surprised. As with the larger popular culture in which we work, the early childhood profession is subject to the whims of fads and trends, fundable issues, and shifting policies around outcome based education.

A poignant moment brought this home to me around five years ago when my colleague Deb Curtis and I were asked to present a three day training for a Head Start program in a small town in the Midwest. As we asked the participants about their goals for the training, most just shrugged their shoulders and were quiet. Finally, someone blurted out, "We're just required to be here. A few years ago the big deal was High/Scope. Then all the training was focused on anti-bias classrooms. Now we're supposed to shift to emergent curriculum. We just go with the flow. Some new thing will come along next year and we'll be required to get training on that." Needless to say, this didn't raise my hopes for meeting any significant outcomes with the three day training we had worked so hard to plan.

Could this "go with the flow" mentality explain the waning interest in anti-bias practices, or is there something else going on? Certainly we haven't erased bias in our programs, nor made them linguistically or culturally relevant for all of the families we serve in our rapidly multiplying multicultural settings. I doubt that many folks can even recall the specific anti-bias goals outlined by Louise Derman-Sparks. Given that we are living in a time of tremendous changes in our demographics, intensified fear and suspicion, hate crimes, cultural clashes, and strong challenges to the value of affirmative action and bilingual education, why is *The Anti-Bias Curriculum* no longer NAEYC's best selling book?

As with any issue, there are layers of complexity involved in training for anti-bias practices, and I suspect some of the passion expressed by its champions, myself included, have put off, if not alienated, people. People don't like to be told they are biased, their classrooms have stereotypes, their multicultural curriculum efforts are a "tourist approach" and tokenize the inclusion of differences. Rather than feel motivated, teachers may become irritated or guilty; directors may just ignore or side step the challenge to re-examine their policies, practices, and environments. I think the anti-bias goals hold the potential to bring about genuine transformation in our diversity work, but what strategies will help us get past our unexamined assumptions, fears, or limited view of ourselves and others?

Anti-bias environments

One of the obvious places to look for bias is in the physical environment, and even before the anti-bias curriculum book was published, creating multicultural environments was an important emphasis in our profession. But inherent in the anti-bias goals is a challenge to go beyond placing diverse images in the environment. The goal is to help children develop a positive identity, critical thinking skills, and the ability to challenge bias and unfairness. To achieve this, programs need to take into account the cultural and linguistic backgrounds of the populations they serve and hire as staff. Each program environment, depending on its composition and context, will look and feel different as it reaches towards culturally relevant, anti-bias goals.

General strategies for culturally relevant, anti-bias environments

■ For your context, regularly conduct discussions about what you need in your physical environment to meet the culturally relevant, anti-bias goals.

■ Be alert to avoid stereotypes and offer images and experiences that counter limited expectations or misunderstandings.

■ Include regular representations of the children's families in the visual and verbal life of your environment.

■ Whether your setting is fairly homogenous or very diverse, think of yourself as a researcher rather than a preacher. Watch and listen for children's efforts to explore their identity, differences, and the meaning of certain cultural practices, holidays, and current events. Have staff discussions to grow your curriculum from these observations.

■ Look for opportunities to acknowledge different perspectives in your activities with children. Continually help the children to practice looking at things in different ways, both in a physical and social sense.

■ Apply the anti-bias goals for the development of your staff as well as the children

---

Anti-bias goals

Foster each child's positive, knowledgeable, and confident self-identity within a cultural context.

Foster each child's comfortable, empathetic interaction with diversity among people.

Foster each child's critical thinking about bias.

Foster each child's ability to stand up for himself or herself and others in the face of bias.

Foster consistency between the families' culture, language, and values, and the curriculum and practices of the program setting.

(Adapted from Louise Derman-Sparks by the Seattle Culturally Relevant Anti-Bias work group)

Organizational culture

It is not only the physical environment, but the social emotional environment or "organizational culture" that must be examined as we undertake culturally relevant, anti-bias goals. How interactions take place, the language used, the systems, policies, and paperwork all shape the larger program environment. Perhaps this is where some of our anti-bias training begins to unnerve folks. The scope of the self-reflection and work to be undertaken can feel overwhelming, calling everything into question.

When we recognize that anti-bias goals are intended to take us beyond teaching tolerance, we can appreciate the need for training that requires us to do some soul searching. Overcoming bias requires that we understand the various forms bias and injustice takes, from assumptions in

---

our thoughts, to our language and actions, and on to the systems and policies which keep bias and inequity in place. The anti-bias challenge is to become active with a transformation in our thinking, our environments, and actions. All of this might be more than what some bargain for as they seek out anti-bias training. On the other hand, nothing less will move us from mere tolerance to genuine transformation.

General strategies for examining organizational culture

■ Stay current and keep deepening your knowledge about your context, the backgrounds of the children, families, and staff.

■ Create opportunities for exchanges around values, assumptions, hopes, and dreams with the children's families and among the staff.

■ Examine your paper work, your language, and your approach to communicating with people. Change systems that make people invisible or suggest only one cultural perspective, language, or family structure is *normal*.

■ Devote time to developing a positive approach to living with and negotiating differences. Practice regularly managing conflicts around simple issues before you are faced with the complex, hot ones.

Clarifying our purpose and training goals

My own journey with anti-bias issues has me moving away from preaching or policing anti-bias efforts toward ones like those reflected in this mission statement I've long held in my files unable to find the source.

The purpose of our work is to uplift the human spirit through transformation of self, communities, and organizations. Through national and international conversations, people are invited to look at their most deeply embedded assumptions. Our goal is to reveal and examine the ideas and fears that keep us apart. (Source Unknown)

Recommended resources

Bisson, J. (1997). *Celebrate. An Anti-Bias Guide to Enjoying Holidays in Early Childhood Programs*. St. Paul, MN: Redleaf Press.

Carter, M. (July 2001). "The Journey to Become a White Ally." *Exchange*, 140(22-24).

Cronin, S., & Masso, C. S. (2003). *Soy Bilingue, Language, Culture, and Young Latino Children./Soy Bilingue, Bicultural Y Orgullosa de Mi Gente*. Center for Linguistic and Cultural Democracy.

Hunt, R. (September 1999). "Making Positive Multicultural Early Childhood Education Happen." *Young Children*.

Lee, E., Menkart, D., & Okazawa-Rey, M. (eds.). (2002). "Tolerance vs. Transformation." *Beyond Heroes and Holidays*, Teaching for Change.

York, S. (2003). *Roots and Wings, Affirming Culture in Early Childhood Programs*. St. Paul, MN: Redleaf Press.

Pelo, A., & Davidson, F. (2000). *That's Not Fair, A Teacher's Guide to Activism with Young Children*. St. Paul, MN: Redleaf Press.

Wolpert, E. (1999). *Start Seeing Diversity: The Basic Guide to an Anti-Bias Classroom*, video and study guide. St. Paul, MN: Redleaf Press.

Margie Carter is the co-author and producer of a number of staff development books and videos. She lives in Seattle, Washington, and travels widely to speak and consult with early childhood programs. Visit www.ecetrainers.com for more information about her work and resources.

How to Stimulate Creativity in Your Staff

by Roger Neugebauer

"In every mind there are widening regions of creativity if once the spark has been allowed to generate the fire."
— Gardner Murphy

Creativity is a vital ingredient of any successful early care and education organization. Creativity is needed in the classroom in planning a responsive curriculum, in designing a stimulating environment, and in providing exciting interactions with the children. The management of a center requires creativity in stretching scant resources, in devising fundraising strategies, and in training and motivating staff. A center must be able to respond creatively to changing populations, changing needs, and changing opportunities.

But can a director truly summon forth a flow of creative ideas from the staff? Aren't there a limited number of creative people in the world and, if your staff doesn't have one, you're out of luck? Management consultant Peter F. Drucker answers that creativity is not in short supply:

"Creativity is not the real problem. There are usually more ideas in any organization than can possibly be put to use . . . . What is lacking is management's willingness to welcome ideas, in fact, solicit them."

Starting with the assumption that creativity is a valuable untapped staff resource, *Exchange* surveyed current management literature for ideas on how to unleash this resource. The following guidelines on how to promote creativity were extracted from those works listed at the end of this article.

Guideline #1.
Clearly communicate the task to the group.

It serves no purpose to get the creative juices of staff members flowing if they are all working on solutions to the wrong problem. At the outset, therefore, it is vital to discuss the problem to be addressed with staff members so that everyone shares a common view of what the group's task is. If the problem is slumping enrollments, for example, everyone should understand that the task is to come up with ideas for recruiting more children. Implicit in this common view is not only a consensus on the specific problem at hand but also a shared understanding of the overall goals and philosophies of the center.

Guideline #2.
Provide group members with rich and varied experiences to draw upon.

Creativity seldom involves the creation of a totally new idea. In their classic treatise on organizational theory, *Organizations*, James March and Herman Simon acknowledged that "most innovations in an organization are a result of borrowing rather than invention." Put another way, creativity involves combining conventional ideas in unconventional ways.

Staff members are more likely to come up with creative combinations of ideas if they have a large store of ideas to draw upon in the first place. According to Gardner Murphy, the first two stages in the creative process are the *immersion in some specific medium that gives delight and fulfillment and the acquisition of experiences which are then consolidated into an ordered pattern*. The director, therefore, needs to provide staff members with opportunities to immerse themselves in the issue at hand and to acquire firsthand experiences with it.

There are many ways in which this can happen. For example, let's say the task at hand is to develop a non-sexist curriculum for the center. The director could pull together all available literature on nonsexist childrearing and education for staff members to read. Staff members could be encouraged to attend workshops and take courses on the subject. They could experiment with nonsexist curriculum ideas in their classrooms. They could visit other centers known for their nonsexist curriculums. And the director could bring in an outside expert to brainstorm with the staff on the subject.

Guideline #3.
Provide staff members with whatever support and encouragement they need.

There is much that a director can do to provide support for the creative efforts of staff members. He can demonstrate confidence in the abilities of staff members by delegating significant responsibility to them to come up with a solution or innovation. A lack of confidence is communicated when the director retains tight control over the entire process.

Support can be provided by protecting the creative process from interference. If some staff members are meeting during nap time to brainstorm about a problem in the center, the director should see to it that they can proceed without interruption. If teachers need to visit other centers or to attend workshops, the director should bring in substitutes when necessary to free them to go out.

Wherever possible, the director should provide budgetary support for the creative process. He should not be a scrooge when it comes to acquiring resource materials needed to explore an issue in depth. He should recognize that new innovations — such as a family child care network for infants or a drop-in program — will not be given a fair trial if they are restricted by too tight a budget at the outset.

Drucker argues that pennywise budgeting can cripple innovative efforts:

"Budgets for ongoing businesses and budgets for innovative efforts must not only be kept separate, they should be treated differently. Instead of asking 'What is the minimum level of support needed?,' ask 'What is the maximum of good people and key resources which can productively be put to work at this stage?'"

Finally, support can be provided in the form of rewards. When staff members are successful in coming up with a creative solution to a problem, their efforts should be rewarded. This reward could take the form of a special commendation in a staff meeting, a special notice to the board of directors or corporate officers, a monetary bonus, or a private word of appreciation.

Guideline #4.
Be realistic in your expectations.

Drucker cautions that "the assumption must be that the majority of innovative efforts will not succeed." If the director or staff members are operating under the unrealistic expectation that every idea they come up with will be an instant winner, they will soon be surprised and discouraged. If those participating in the process recognize at the outset that maybe nine out of every ten ideas they come up with will not reach fruition, they will be more patient in waiting for those rare successes.

Guideline #5.
Foster a permissive atmosphere for crazy ideas.

One rule in brainstorming sessions is that participants are not allowed to make negative comments about ideas proposed by other participants. The reason for this is that if participants

have their ideas shot down in the group, they will become more defensive and stop offering ideas at all or offer only cautious noncontroversial ideas which they know won't be attacked. With negative judgments being withheld, participants are more likely to offer a wide range of ideas.

A director interested in tapping the creative resources of staff members needs to develop among center staff the same openness to ideas which exists in a brainstorming session. Staff members need to feel that their suggestions and ideas are welcomed and valued. They should not be reluctant to share their thoughts out of fear they will be ridiculed, criticized, or ignored.

The director should provide staff members with multiple channels for offering their ideas. Ideas could be sought in staff meetings with a brainstorming format. For those intimidated in group discussions, the director may want to solicit their views in private conversations. Others may not want to share their opinions in public at all but may need the impersonal avenue of a suggestion box.

Guideline #6.
Expose ideas proposed to critical examination.

The vacation from criticism should not last forever. Once staff members are secure enough to risk unlimited speculation, there needs to be a point where ideas proposed are evaluated with a critical eye. "The creative process," explains William J. J. Gordon, "stems from the total personalities, and an attempt to deny the critical element can have no lasting productive effect."

However, there are constructive and nonconstructive ways to offer criticism. For example, if in a staff meeting all suggestions for redesigning the outdoor play area are being reviewed, the tendency of group members may be to select the best suggestion and to reject all the others. In this process, the useful elements or germs of ideas in the nonwinners are often missed.

To avoid this *all-or-nothing* criticism, a number of techniques can be employed. One is to require group members to point out the good aspects of a proposal as well as the negative ones when offering criticism. A related approach is to expect critics to offer suggestions on how they would modify a rejected proposal. Finally, an opponent of an idea could be expected to offer an alternative to the idea he is opposing.

Guideline #7.
Allow staff members to concentrate on problems that especially interest them.

According to Harry Levinson, an organization is best served when it "permits people to seize and develop those challenges and problems which most excite their curiosity." A director, for example, could hold a staff meeting at which all staff members brainstorm about the center's major problems to be solved and opportunities to be seized. From this discussion a priority list of tasks to be addressed could be compiled, and each staff member could be allowed to choose one or two tasks to focus attention on.

One consequence of this approach, Levinson notes, is that staff members may be interested in an issue that "may not at the moment be of major concern to the organization." This drawback is compensated for by the fact that "the freedom to follow one's interest stimulates a flow of ideas." This flow of ideas on a range of issues would be far more useful to the center in the long run than the trickle of ideas that might result if all staff members were required to be

creative about a crucial problem that did not interest most of them.

Guideline #8.
Allow staff members to proceed at their own pace and in their own way.

Individuals cannot turn their creative process on and off like a faucet. Everyone has their own pattern or pace for evoking creativity. One person gets a mental block about problems while on the job but finds that ideas come to him in a flood when he is jogging. Another has no success until late at night when he relaxes in his favorite chair with a cup of tea. Most people need to take a mental vacation somewhere in the process — they need to follow a period of intense immersion in a problem with a totally new activity where the conscious mind focuses on something different.

As often as not, the solution that did not come when a person was deliberately trying to think of it will pop into his mind when he is thinking about something else. This unpredictable, highly individualized nature of the creative process must be taken into account by a director seeking to make it happen.

Guideline #9.
Don't foil brainstorming sessions with preliminary termination.

Guideline #8 applies to the creative process as it occurs in individuals, and Guideline #9 applies to the creative process as it occurs in groups. The rules for these two settings differ considerably. In a group setting, it becomes more important to force the process along somewhat.

After an hour or so of intense concentration in a brainstorming session, many staff members will be showing signs of fatigue and may look for an end to the session or at least a prolonged coffee break. Gordon argues,

however, that generally such a break should be avoided. He contends that it takes a long time for the creative process to get rolling. To take a break in midstream "would interrupt the continuity of thought . . . and would allow the subconscious imaginative energy to congeal." To reach a satisfactory conclusion, Gordon finds, brainstorming sessions must often continue for three hours.

One means of combatting fatigue without terminating the meeting is comedy. When the energy level is drooping, a group member can make a satirical or offbeat suggestion to allow the discussion to digress from the intense level for a few minutes. According to Gordon, "after a few minutes of laughter group members are usually ready again for rigorous and energetic performance."

Gordon also sees some advantage to fatigue setting in. It can force participants to let their guard down and to abandon themselves to taking longer chances. Group members may start swinging for the fences. Such a swing can be the culmination of protracted imaginative effort — not merely a wild blow, but a highly concentrated mental act tending to reveal a creative solution.

Guideline #10.
Don't underestimate the value of success.

Nothing will help the flow of creativity along better than some early and continuing successes. If a director sets out to foster a creative spirit, staff members may initially react with disinterest or pessimism. If the group experiences an early success — if it comes up with a creative solution to a problem — this early uncertainty may be replaced by interest and excitement. If success is long in coming, the uncertainty may deteriorate into frustration and cynicism.

With this in mind, directors might want to focus on problems of minor magnitude early on to improve the likelihood of success. Gordon also suggests that, until the initial success is realized, no meeting should end on a note of defeat. The director may want to hold off on some promising suggestions until the end of a session if it is not going well. Or he may want to summarize at the end all the promising leads which were brought up during the session.

Having tasted early success, staff members usually will be more patient in waiting for additional victories. But these victories must occur from time to time if participants are going to maintain faith in the effort. One frequent shortcoming is that lots of creative ideas are proposed, but none of them are ever implemented. Murphy identifies *hammering out* as the final stage in the creative process. When the group comes up with a creative solution to a problem, its work is not done. The solution must be worked out in detail, adopted to the center's exact needs, and implemented. The creative process does not end in success when the solution is created, but only when the problem is in fact solved.

References

Drucker, P. F. (1974). *Management: Tasks, Responsibilities, Practices.* New York: Harper and Row.

Drucker, P. F. (May-June 1964). "The Big Power of Little Ideas." *Harvard Business Review.*

Gordon, W. J. J. (November-December 1956). "Operational Approach to Creativity." *Harvard Business Review.*

Levinson, H. (1968). *The Exceptional Executive.* Cambridge: Harvard University Press.

March, J., & Simon, H. (1958). *Organizations.* New York: John Wiley and Sons.

Murphy, G. (1958). *Human Potentialities.* New York: Basic Books.

Helping Teachers Grow: Confronting Inappropriate Teaching Behavior

by Kay Albrecht

"I have told Mary again and again that she needs to get down at children's eye level and she still doesn't do it!" It seems so simple. You know what you want to have happen. You share that information with the person who can make it happen. And nothing happens.

Although the center director's job has many frustrating aspects, confronting inappropriate teaching behaviors in a manner which produces change is an ongoing challenge. Many a director has been frustrated when her guidance to teachers about appropriate and inappropriate teaching skills fails to have the desired impact. Let's take a look at a design for helping teachers grow by confronting inappropriate teaching behaviors in a way that is most likely to produce change — and, in the process, improve the teacher's skill and the center's program quality.

Confrontation usually has a negative connotation. In many minds, it is associated with conflict. But confrontation is different from conflict. Constructive confrontation is a way to help calibrate perceptions of one's own strengths or limitations (in this case in teaching competence) with the perceptions of others (either supervisors, clients, or peers). When approached correctly, confrontation can be healthy, stimulating, and change-producing.

Five steps to growth

Confrontation which results in growth has five steps. First — identify the behavior you want changed. Nailing down the problem by specifying which specific behavior you want a teacher to change can be difficult — but if you can't do it, you are not ready to confront. Second — identify and describe how you want the new behavior to look. Specifying the change you want is the goal of this step. Third — identify how the change is to be brought about. This critical third step is what causes many to flounder. Developing the plan for bringing about change and identifying who will play what role in facilitating the change is difficult. Fourth — determine how the change will be measured. Consider including specifications about time, quantity, and quality. And fifth — identify how successful change will be measured, by whom, and when.

An example to illustrate the steps:

1. Identify the problem. Mary doesn't get down on children's eye level (an important teacher competency which facilitates positive interactions among children and teachers).

2. Identify and describe how the new behavior should look. When interacting with children, Mary will bend over, stoop, get down on the floor, or sit on the hassocks which bring her down to the children's eye level.

3. Describe how the change will be brought about. Every time I pass Mary's classroom door and think that she should be sitting, bending, or stooping to interact, I will signal Mary by pulling on my ear. The purpose of the signal is to make Mary aware of where she is in relation to children.

4. Determine how the change will be measured — in time, quantity, and quality. After two weeks of signaling, I expect Mary to be bending over, stooping down, or sitting while interacting with children at least half the number of times I pass by her classroom. After a month, Mary should be bending over, stooping down, or sitting while interacting with children on three out of four times.

5. Determine how success will be measured. When Mary is at children's eye level during 75% of her interactions (based on a one hour observation) or when she no longer needs signaling to sensitize her to where she is in relation to the children in her classroom (she is at eye level when interacting 75% of the times I pass her classroom), we will assume that Mary has mastered this skill.

Prerequisites to constructive confrontation

In order to help teachers grow, it must be clear to everyone involved what teaching competence means. The best way to make sure everyone knows is to have a clear program philosophy statement from which a list of philosophically compatible teaching competencies or skills are identified and then used in self and supervisor evaluation.

To find out if your philosophy is clear and understandable, ask your teachers to write it down for you in their own words. Then ask them to make a list of skills that teachers who follow the philosophy must have in order to implement a quality program. The results will give you insight into the clarity of your philosophy and the ability of others to interpret what the philosophy means.

Constructive confrontation works best when it begins early in the

---

Making Constructive Confrontation Work

- Break things down into manageable components. It is ineffective to start with "You're a bad teacher." Pick one skill to focus on at a time, allow a reasonable time for improvement, then pick another, and so forth.

- Pick discreet skills that can be taught. For a good list of *teachable* skills, see "Self-Evaluation — Early Childhood Teacher," (*Exchange*, April 1989). Stick to skills that are *teachable*. Avoid personality traits or personal style issues.

- Start with teaching behaviors that really matter. Skills that focus on interaction among teachers and children, curriculum, and parent-teacher interaction are some of the skills that make the most difference.

- Focus on outcomes. The process of change will happen more readily if the outcome is specified while the path for accomplishing the goal allows for flexibility, creativity, individuality, and spontaneity.

---

teacher-director relationship. If you have a staff member who has been with you for three years and has never been given any feedback on her teaching competence, it will be much harder to get the process of change started.

Constructive confrontation of teaching skill deficits requires that equal attention be given to skill strengths. This does not mean beginning confrontation sessions by identifying one or two teaching skills that are a part of the teacher skill repertoire. It means regular and frequent positive feedback as skills are demonstrated.

When skill strengths are recognized, the next step of working on skill deficits emerges naturally.

Kay Albrecht, Ph.D., is the former executive director of HeartsHome Early Learning Center, Houston, Texas, and senior partner in Innovations in Early Childhood Education. Her specialties include teacher training and curriculum development. Her latest book, **Innovations in Infant Curriculum**, *is in press with Gryphon House. In 2000, she served as the academic dean of the World Forum.*

Planning Staff Meetings

by Margie Carter

One of the biggest challenges early care and education programs face is finding a suitable time, space, and budget for all staff meetings. With all the varying work shifts in a program, getting everyone to attend a meeting and paying them for this time requires a logistical genius, not to mention slippery budget configurations.

Surprisingly, large agencies often seem to have a better time of it than smaller programs do. School districts, Ys, and multi-service agencies tend to plan their annual calendars with staff development and meeting days in mind, and they don't renege in spite of the inconvenience this may cause the families they serve. Large or small, the programs most successful in carving out regular meeting time for staff set their calendars for the year and have persuasive rationales and policies for parents, along with clear expectations for staff attendance.

Some do this with a consistently scheduled early closure once a month, while others close quarterly for a staff development day. When programs hold evening all staff meetings, they often make use of a floating substitute for the week of the meeting so that each staff member gets comp time for these required extra meeting hours. A consortium of early childhood program directors serving low income families decided to collectively close their programs the last few days of the week before the Labor Day weekend

to do some individual program and community-wide staff training.

However we configure it, the gyrations required to gather our staff together for a meeting creates an imperative to consider this time as precious and to use it well. In my view, thoughtful planning and organization of our meeting time and space should parallel the process we want the teachers to bring to their work with children and families. The *process* we use in gathering our staff together can be as significant for our staff development as any *content* we might hope to cover during the meeting. When directors create a thoughtful model for adult learning, teachers experience first hand the deep respect and thoughtful planning we want them to offer the children.

Be clear about the purpose and structure of your meetings

Sometimes we gather our staff together to review important program considerations, make decisions, or strategize on

how to best support a child, family, or staff member. Other times our meetings have the structure of a workshop focused on a particular topic, for instance, health and safety practices, promoting literacy, or child guidance. There are occasions when we gather together primarily for social time, perhaps celebrating an accomplishment, holiday, or person we want to honor.

It seems a terrible misuse of our precious gatherings to use them primarily for the business details of staff schedules, reminders of regulations, or important announcements. This information could be better delegated to smaller team meetings, bulletins, or routing slip memos. There are occasions when staff input or involvement in important decisions works best in a meeting where all points of view can be heard and differences negotiated. (Paula Jorde Bloom's little book *Circle of Influence: Implementing Shared Decision Making and Participative Management* offers great ideas for how to think about this.)

In our book *The Visionary Director*, Deb Curtis and I offer a triangle framework for thinking through and organizing your work as a director into three comprehensive areas: managing and overseeing resources, systems, policies, standards; teaching and coaching with a focus on your staff as learners; and building and supporting community within your program and between your program and the wider community. You can plan staff meetings with the triangle framework in mind.

Managing and overseeing tasks for meetings:

- Creating a system for agenda development and the meeting structure
- Arranging the schedule and environment
- Creating the development of and coaching system for your Code of Conduct or Ground Rules for Meeting Behaviors
- Managing a system for recording and documenting meeting discussions, decisions, and activities
- Monitoring the group process and dynamics
- Tracking responsibilities, decisions, tasks, odds and ends
- Using evaluation systems and planning needed changes

Teaching and coaching tasks for meetings:

- Using staff meetings for learning and development (rather than business announcements)
- Focusing time with hands on, meaningful learning experiences
- Providing for individual learning styles and collaborative thinking experiences
- Coaching with developmental stages and milestones in mind
- Using facilitative questions to promote self-reflection

Building and supporting community tasks for meetings:

- Creating a climate for all voices to be heard and respected
- Providing opportunities to get connected through shared experiences
- Practicing the recognition and valuing of different perspectives and communication styles and negotiating differences
- Exploring ways to connect with the wider community
- Celebrating significant events

Planning meetings for learning and connecting

You can provide effective training during staff meetings if your primary goal is to offer a learning process for the adults, rather than trying to convey information. Time devoted to active learning in staff meetings conveys the importance you place on thinking and growing, and develops your program as a learning community for adults as well as children.

Strategy:
Do skits rather than announcements

I saw a wonderful example of a director turning *reminders* into a playful learning and community building activity. Concerned that some new staff hadn't been working during the summer in her program, director Susie Eisman at Hilltop Children's Center wrote headings of key topics she wanted to review on pieces of paper, i.e., field trip safety, summer sun health issues, playground first aid, communications with families. Small clusters of staff members were given one of these topics, asked to brainstorm a list of concerns to plan for, and then weave these into a skit to present to the whole staff.

Rather than a yawn-filled hour of a long list of guidelines, teachers were treated to a fun-filled time of discovering their creativity, shared knowledge, and values. Months later they were still talking about that hilarious way Lisa played the devil's voice in Jason's ear trying to get him to ignore the safety guidelines for transporting children on field trips, and how Kit reminded the child stung by a bee how to avoid trauma for the bee as well.

Strategy:
Explore different values

Teachers benefit from examining and naming the influences on their own values and preferred practices. It is useful to do this in a context stripped of a *right or wrong* tone. A simple way to do this is to write on separate pieces of paper possible opposing viewpoints on policies and practices and then post them around the room. Ask everyone to find one viewpoint they wish to discuss, go to that paper, and talk with others there. They don't have to agree with the viewpoint, but they should have strong sentiments they want to discuss. Possible ideas for the papers include: children should call adults by their first names; children should primarily be offered limited choices and non-negotiable guidelines from adults; children should have to try at least one bite of all food served; parents should be immediately told when their children break a rule.

In the debriefing discussion following the talk at the different papers, acknowledge that sometimes teachers are asked to carry out practices different from their own belief systems, or there may be a difference between a family's practice and that of the program. Exploring the values and belief systems underlying practices with children can result in new learning and a willingness to accommodate a different viewpoint without judgment or negation.

Strategy:
Invite neighborhood kindergarten teachers and principals

In today's climate of outcomes-based education and high-stakes testing, it is easy for schools and early childhood programs to point a finger at each other. Why not, instead, try to build a relationship and some mutual understandings between your staff and that of the schools your children typically move on to? Invite the kindergarten teachers and principals to come hear stories of how your children are learning through play. Share documentation of in-depth projects, transcriptions of children's conversations, and other evidence of their learning process. Ask to hear the teachers' and principals' frustrations and concerns and ideas for building stronger connections between your programs. Consider including parents and some of your graduates to contribute to this meeting as well.

Strategy:
Do a self-assessment of recent meetings

To explore this idea of having your staff meetings parallel what you want the teachers to be doing with the children, reflect on your last three meetings. Creating three columns on a paper with the dates of each meeting as the headers, quickly jot down the agenda for each and a summary of how time was spent, the tone, focus, and primary voices that were heard. Consider these questions as well:

■ Was the space well-organized, comfortable, and inviting?
■ What kinds of choices did the staff have about how time was spent?
■ In what ways were people able to deepen their relationships and experience being part of a community?
■ How were staff given opportunities to construct their knowledge about something worth learning?
■ In what ways was their learning or experience made visible?

Looking over your answers, do you feel your staff had a meaningful learning experience and deepened their connections with each other, the program philosophy and vision, or possibly the value of their work to the wider community?

Margie Carter has co-authored with Deb Curtis numerous early childhood books and staff training videos which are described on their web site at www.ecetrainers.com.

Chapter 4

Motivating
and
Supervising Staff

12 Reasons People Love to Work for You

by Roger Neugebauer

"The well director doesn't work to make people love her, but makes people love to work for her."

I proposed this maxim in an article, "The Well Director," in the March 1987 issue of *Exchange*. Since then, a number of people (two) have said, "Well, that sounds just peachy, but how do you make people love to work for you in real life?"

So I've been keeping my eye on the directors of centers where teacher turnover is low, trying to figure out what they are doing right. Based on these observations, here are 12 practices you can implement to motivate people to stay — 12 reasons people will love to work for you.

1
You believe in people from day one.

With the shrinking supply of qualified teachers, there is a tendency to be pessimistic about the potential of the people we hire. This pessimism can result in a self-fulfilling prophecy: we don't expect high performance; so we don't make an effort to encourage high performance; and, in the end, we don't see high performance.

You can't manipulate people like puppets. They alone have the power to decide whether they will work hard.

However, your attitude about a person can have a significant dampening or buoying impact on their self-confidence. When you believe a person has the potential to succeed, and when you believe that a person has a desire to succeed, your support can make a difference.

2
You build on people's strengths.

You will never find the perfect teacher, or cook, or bookkeeper, or bus driver (or spouse, for that matter). All of us have our short-comings. However, we don't hire people because of their weaknesses. We hire them because we see some talent, some experience, or some trait which is a strength that we need.

To help new employees succeed on the job, you need to focus on the reasons you hired them. Time devoted to building on people's strengths is

time well invested. Time spent in dwelling on people's weaknesses is, more often than not, time wasted.

There always will be occasions when you must affirmatively deal with malperformance which is directly affecting the quality of your program — conflict, absenteeism, inappropriate discipline, etc. However, focusing all your energy on people's short-comings results mostly in frustration, anger, and alienation (anyone with teenagers can relate to this).

One director I visited likes to get things off on the right foot by finding something a new employee will succeed in their first day. She assigns them some specific activity or task that employs a skill or training that they possess already.

Betty Jones, from Pacific Oaks, suggests that the early training teachers receive should build on the skills a person brings to the job, even though that may not be the most important thing they need to know to do their job. If you encourage a new employee to improve on an area of strength, they will be less threatened because they are on turf that is comfortable and familiar to them. Then, as they feel rewarded by their improvement in a "safe" area, you can gradually nudge them to grow in areas where they may feel less secure.

3
You provide people with feedback.

One of the most frequent complaints I hear from teachers is that they do not receive feedback about their efforts. They do not know if the director thinks they are doing a good job overall, or if the director even cares.

According to management guru Peter Drucker, what employees most need to improve their performance is an abundance of objective, timely feedback on the results of their performance. In well-functioning centers, the director places a high priority on encouraging staff to provide feedback to each other, in training staff on how to give feedback, and in providing time and tools for all types of feedback systems.

4
You view people's welfare as a high priority.

When it comes to worker compensation, we all sing the right tune. We all lament the low wages and benefits our teachers receive. But passionate speeches don't pay the rent.

There are no easy solutions to the compensation dilemma. No knight in shining armor is going to charge in and save the day — not the federal government, not employers, and not labor unions.

The solution will primarily come from tough choices and hard compromises made one center at a time. A director who is truly committed to making progress on the compensation issue will be educating parents and raising fees, and will be actively exploring creative solutions to improving benefits.

Teachers lose faith in a director who decries low wages but refuses to raise fees for fear of upsetting parents. The bottom line is that teachers' commitment will be impacted by whether or not they perceive that you truly do place a high priority on their welfare.

5
You build team spirit.

Clare Cherry, in addition to all her writing and speaking, actually directed a early childhood center in San Bernardino, California. In interviewing prospective teachers, she informed them if they were to work at her center they would be required to accept responsibility for helping all the teachers improve.

Teachers at Clare's center were expected to share ideas, to give each other feedback, to solve problems together, and to provide each other support. She viewed teamwork as an essential ingredient of an excellent program. And for team spirit to flower, it requires such commitment from the top to make it happen.

You need to be continually exploring ways to encourage cooperative efforts, whether it means rotating the chair at staff meetings, regularly conducting brainstorming sessions to attack center problems, or taking the entire staff on a retreat. Team building needs to be a conscious activity promoted by the director, attended to by the director, and rewarded by the director.

6
You inspire commitment.

One of the responsibilities of the leader in any organization is to serve as the keeper of the faith. You need to have a vision for your organization that gives meaning to your work and inspires you to act.

If you have such a vision, this will not only inspire you, but it should infect everyone who works in the organization. Directors I have observed who are committed to a vision exude intensity and excitement which energizes everyone in their centers.

When people are committed to the goals of an organization, they will work hard to ensure that these goals are achieved. This is much more powerful then trying to build people's commitment to you as an individual.

7
You set high standards.

In the very best centers I visit, the directors have an unflagging commitment to high performance. Even when crises seem to be breaking out all over, these directors do not allow these frustrations to serve as an excuse for letting up on quality.

Achieving high standards in a early childhood center is indeed a very imposing challenge. Pressure to maintain these standards can understandably put a heavy burden on all staff. However, these frustrations are far outweighed by the feeling of pride that comes from working in a first class organization.

8
You remove obstacles to people's success.

The most effective directors I see do not view themselves as making things happen by sitting atop the chain of command issuing orders and making inspirational speeches. Rather, they view themselves as servants to the team.

These directors see their job as helping teachers succeed by getting them the resources they need to grow and perform. They take seriously the responsibility of removing obstacles that get in the way of people doing their jobs, whether it be replacing equipment that's worn out or reorganizing a staffing structure that doesn't work.

9
You encourage people to take risks.

We all view ourselves as open, supportive, and encouraging. But sometimes our intentions are belied by our actions.

We may encourage staff to be creative, yet convey through body language a sense of disapproval when they try a new activity and it fails. We may ask people for their solutions to a center problem, but criticize any suggestions they make.

If you expect your people to act creatively, you have to send a strong message that you support them. You must praise people for taking risks. You need to thank people for having the courage to disagree with you. You must provide a rich environment of books, materials, trips, and workshops to keep people thinking and growing. And, most importantly, you should demonstrate that you are willing to take risks yourself.

10
You make working fun.

One of the most consistent features of centers where teachers love to work is a relaxed, happy atmosphere. Early care and education is hard work with serious implications. But no one can thrive without laughter or joy.

11
You cultivate professional pride.

A disquieting aspect of all the media attention early care and education has received in recent years has been the "crisis" mode of much of the coverage. Documentary after documentary, and article after article, decries how horrible child care conditions are in this country (especially when compared, over and over again, with the faultless Swedish child care system).

This coverage may serve a purpose in focusing attention on the need for additional resources to assist low income families and to improve working conditions. However, it also tends to disparage the valiant efforts of those working in centers today.

Isabella Graham (the director featured on the cover of the November 1990 issue of *Exchange*) opened the first child care center in the nation 162 years ago. In that issue, we included a list of the 50 oldest centers in the nation which included 21 centers which have been in operation over 100 years.

Child care is not a recent fad or new profession struggling to get its act together. We have a long, proud tradition of caring. We make it possible for our nation's economy to function. We are providing a nurturing, stimulating start in life for millions of children. Your staff should take pride in being a part of the early childhood profession.

12
You help people see results.

Lilian Katz — in an article, "On Teaching," in the February 1990 issue of *Exchange* — noted that every semester there will be two or three of her students who reveal that a single teacher, by showing concern or encouragement, saved their psychological lives. Katz concludes: "Just think how many children that adds up to over a career of teaching . . . it could be more than 100 people. That's a lot of lives to make a real difference to."

As a director, the most effective way you can get teachers hooked on continuing in your center is to help them see the real impact they are having on the lives of children. You can do this by training teachers to be better observers so they can see the children progress, by encouraging teachers to give each other feedback on the changes they observe, and, foremost, by encouraging parents to share their joy over the progress their children are making.

Knowing that you were responsible for helping a shy child come out of his shell or an overly aggressive child calm down is a type of reward that very few professions can offer.

William Franklin, speaking at an *Exchange* conference in New Orleans, quoted the remarks made by Pericles to his troops, noting that he could just as well have been addressing early childhood professionals:

"What you leave behind is not what is engraved in stone monuments, but what is woven into the lives of others."

There are many great reasons for working in early childhood, not the least of which is the real difference we can make in the lives of the children and families we serve.

What Do Teachers Need Most From Their Directors?

by Margie Carter

"Perceptions are powerful regulators of behavior that can influence teachers' level of commitment to a center. In fact, people's perceptions of events may be more important than reality because individuals act according to their interpretation of events."
— Paula Jorde Bloom, *Circle of Influence*

Over the last eight months, I've been doing an informal research project. Nothing scientific. No statistical analysis. Just keeping my ears finely tuned and asking a few focused questions as I work with early childhood teachers at their program sites and in seminars at conferences. There is now an established process called "participatory research," but I can't claim to have been even that systematic in my inquiry. Mostly, I've just been trying to carefully listen for what management styles, dispositions, and skills engender confidence and respect from staff toward their director. Are there particular philosophies, policies, decision-making and communication systems that influence teachers to stay at their workplace longer, despite inadequate salaries and benefits?

What I've consistently heard from teachers reflects the research behind several important publications in our field:

■ Paula Jorde Bloom's two books, *A Great Place to Work: Improving Conditions for Staff in Young Children's Programs* and *Circle of Influence: Implementing Shared Decision Making and Participative Management*

■ The Center for the Child Care Workforce (CCW) publication, *Creating Better Child Care Jobs: Model Work Standards for Teaching Staff in Center-Based Child Care*

Bloom discusses her research on how the interplay between people and the environment, and between work attitudes and group dynamics, supports the professionalism of an organization. In discussing the concept of organizational climate, she says: "Although it is not clear whether climate or satisfaction comes first, job satisfaction seems to be higher in schools with relatively open climates. These climates are characterized by a sense of belonging, many opportuni-

ties to interact, autonomy, and upward influence." (1997)

More recently, through the efforts of the Center for the Child Care Workforce, early childhood program staff themselves have been developing an assessment tool, the *Model Work Standards*, which highlights the components of work environments that are linked to quality for children in our programs. This tool is a welcome addition to our field and substantiates Bloom's point:

"One valuable insight gained during an assessment of employee attitudes about their work environment is the sharper understanding of where perceptions differ between administrators and employees. One of the more common findings, for example, is that directors often believe they give far more feedback to their staff than their teachers perceive they get. Another common difference is found in the directors' and staff's perceptions regarding staff involvement in decisions about practices to be followed in the center . . . directors typically rate the climate more favorably than do teachers." (1997)

The impetus for my own investigation into what teachers want from their directors stems from continually hearing examples of differing perceptions between directors and staff in their rating of the work environment. It strikes me that because directors work so hard and under such stress, they are sometimes reluctant to welcome staff perspectives on what needs changing if there aren't resources or time to commit to an issue. However, I've discovered that when directors welcome feedback on how the work environment feels, they unlock the potential for creative problem solving. A tool such as the *Model Work Standards* helps directors clearly see where their program should be headed. As with accreditation criteria, it can serve as a weather gauge for the organizational climate and a concrete reference point for budgeting and/or grant writing.

In *A Great Place to Work*, Paula Jorde Bloom is instructive about the dimensions of an organizational climate that need tending to in our early childhood programs. She is also quite persuasive in *Circle of Influence*, detailing the value of shared decision making and participative management. What she says in these two publications outlining her research is what I have been hearing in my informal, yet careful listening work with teachers.

As I ask, "What do teachers need most from their directors," either as a direct question to them or as I focus my listening and watching, I consistently hear a call for tending to the physical, social, and emotional environment of the program. These are my categories for their ideas, different from but interrelated to the research message from Bloom and the Center for the Child Care Workforce.

Offer genuine respect and trust

The words "trust" and "respect" easily roll off our tongues, and our heads nod when we hear them, but what do these words look like in action? Teachers say they usually feel respected when someone really listens to them, trying to understand and be responsive, rather than just placating. Some talk about "being trusted to succeed," even if they falter or "goof up." But they are quick to add that respect and trust means being given the time, support, and tools they need, not leaving them alone to sink or swim but neither hovering or micro-managing. "When I'm really listened to and taken seriously, I feel validated and respected." Others use the word "empowered" along with trust and respect. One teacher commented: "Empowerment can be a bogus word. No one can give you your power, but they can disempower you, taking away your self-trust and respect. When your director trusts you, you are motivated to use your power to learn and get it right."

Some teachers claim that directors only show trust and respect to staff members who agree with them. This clearly undermines what Bloom refers to as "collegiality" in naming ten important dimensions in an organizational climate. Posting a sign or announcing "We will all respect each other here" irritates some teachers. You can't mandate trust and respect. These feelings have to be developed over time with accumulated experiences to confirm or counter our initial impressions.

Trust comes more quickly when we work from both our heads and our hearts. As we become clear about our values and ideas, and learn to communicate them with a blend of honesty and empathy, respect for different points of view can grow. We don't have to become best friends to trust each other, but we do have to have mutual respect and be able to count on each other if genuine trust is to grow and thrive.

Work with a vision

It's striking to hear teachers describe the contrast between directors who work with a vision and those who settle for how things are. The word "vision" isn't always used, but they excitedly describe how their director really inspired them to work at the center, how "she's usually got a twinkle in her eye," is always "showing us pictures or little quotes to expand our thinking," or "keeps her eye on the prize even when our budget comes up short." Perhaps some of this is related to the dimension Bloom calls "innovation" or "goal consensus." Teachers can sense when directors are moving their program forward toward a bigger dream, even as they are thwarted by the crisis of the week. The climate is quite different than one limited to following the rules and regulations or resigning the program to the limitations of the moment.

Teachers acknowledge that directors with big dreams can sometimes overlook the trees for the forest. They can get caught up in grant writing, meetings in the community, or calls and visits to their legislators and neglect a child, parent, or teacher requiring immediate attention, film waiting to be developed, or a promised professional training opportunity. Most teachers don't just want to be kept informed of where the director is heading; they want a role in shaping a vision for the program. When they are offered this involvement, their energy and talents can be tapped and their commitment to the program grows. This is a very different experience for staff than merely delegating responsibility for some tasks the director can't get to. Teachers not only want to work with visionary directors, they want to dream and plan along with them.

Share the decision-making process

"I hate it when our director has made a decision and then goes through the motions of asking for our input. It's a waste of time and makes me resentful." CCW's *Model Work Standards* have several components which address this common sentiment from teachers. Their categories of communication, team building, and staff meetings, as well as decision making and problem solving, offer important descriptions of what teachers deem as necessary in a quality work environment. Bloom, in turn, has devoted a book in her *Director's Toolbox* series to the topic of implementing shared decision making and participative management. *Circle of Influence* outlines principles and values that support collaborative decision making and offers guidelines for determining decision-making processes and avoiding pitfalls. Bloom says:

"It is not enough to embrace the beliefs and values surrounding participation. Organizational structures and processes must be adapted so that staff and other stakeholders have the power and capacity to participate actively in decision-making ventures."

Teachers want clarity in the process for making decisions about things which impact their ability to do their jobs well. Many want more than that and are eager to be mentored in understanding the big picture and learning consensus-building skills. They want their directors to offer strong leadership in getting all voices to the table. Teachers are intuitively clear about the difference between autocratic and democratic leadership, often mentioning the way their director succeeds or fails to facilitate the group dynamics so that everyone has power and input and teachers cultivate their own leadership skills.

Reject a scarcity mentality

Related to working with vision is the idea that teachers don't want their directors to just settle for how things are. They need to see and hear their directors pushing ahead with improvements in their compensation and working conditions.

A wonderful example of this can be found in an article by Carl Sussman, "Out of the Basement: Discovering the Value of Child Care Facilities." Sussman's specific focus is a story of a Head Start director with a vision to create an inspiring new building, but the lessons for directors are even broader — what I call rejecting a scarcity mentality. Sussman puts it this way: "To conserve energy for the educational tasks at hand, many teachers and administrators learn to live with modest expectations. They avoid disappointment by sacrificing their vision . . . (they) need to cultivate the cognitive dissonance of living with inadequate facilities while harboring an ambitious vision that could sustain a greatly enhanced program."

Teachers have many ways of describing the scarcity mentality they experience in their directors, be it excessive penny pinching, power holding as if there's only so much available, failure to network and connect with outside resources, or repeated responses to new ideas with a "They won't let us" or "No way! We can't afford it." They describe directors who inspire and sustain them with contrasting responses such as "Let's see how we could make that work" or "You're pushing me beyond what I know how to do but I want to take up that challenge."

Tend to the physical environment

The typical early childhood program is situated in a less than ideal space with more limitations than we know what to do with. In his article, Sussman describes our situation this way:

"Years of budget balancing and widespread acceptance of inadequate facilities has desensitized providers to their environment and created chronically low expectations." In his article, he goes on to describe how the physical quality of a center can influence the way teachers interact with children and has the potential to reduce staff turnover rates. Indeed, one of the component areas of the *Model Work Standards* is the physical setting, where what teachers need for the children and themselves is delineated.

Most early childhood programs don't draw on the research from other professions about the impact of space, light, and color on behavior. We often furnish our programs with little attention to aesthetics or imagination. Across the country, many early childhood programs have begun to look alike, a mini replica of an early childhood catalog. Usually there are child-sized tables and chairs, primary colors, an abundance of plastic materials, commercial toys, and bulletin board displays. You have to search to find soft or natural elements, places where adults as well as children can feel cozy, alone or with a friend. The smell of disinfectant often floats in the air. Have we forgotten how a cluttered or tattered environment quickly seeps into our psyche? Do we know how a sterile and antiseptic climate shapes our soul?

Caregivers, teachers, and children are spending the bulk of their waking hours living their lives together in our programs. The way we organize the space, create traffic and communication patterns, furnish and decorate all affect the experience people have in our buildings. When I listen for what teachers want from their directors, there is always something about improving the physical environment. In our book, *The Visionary Director*, Deb Curtis and I offer scores of ideas for creating an environment for adults that not only meets their needs but parallels what we want them to be providing for children: softness; beauty; order; reflections of their interests, culture, and home life; things to discover and invent with; a place for personal belongings; and so forth. When directors give attention to the physical environment, it nourishes everyone involved and creates an on-going sense of possibilities.

Walk your talk

Again and again, teachers tell me there's nothing worse than a director who doesn't walk her talk. Promises without follow through, martyring oneself rather than modeling self-care, making excuses rather than making things happen are all behaviors that erode trust and respect. If you say you want more diversity in your program, then you must change the things that are keeping your

program homogeneous. When you articulate a vision for your program, you must grow your way into it with how you set priorities and goals, create an environment and organizational culture, harness resources, and conduct human interactions. Listening to what teachers need from their directors can be a superficial endeavor or one which deepens understandings and broadens possibilities. It also contributes to a more stable, committed staff.

References and recommended resources

Bloom, P. J. (1997). *A great place to work: Improving conditions for staff in young children's programs* (Rev. ed.). Washington, DC: NAEYC.

Bloom, P. J. (2000). *Circle of influence: Implementing shared decision making and participative management.* New Horizons, PO Box 863, Lake Forest, IL 60045-0863, (847) 295-8131.

Carter, M., & Curtis, D. (1998). *The visionary director: A handbook for dreaming, organizing, & improvising in your center.* St Paul, MN: Redleaf Press.

The Center for the Child Care Workforce. (1998). *Creating better child care jobs: Model work standards for teaching staff in center-based child care.* The Center for the Child Care Workforce, 733 15th Street NW, Suite 1037, Washington, DC 20005-2112, (202) 737-7700, fax: (202) 737-0370 (ccw@ccw.org).

Sussman, C. (1998). "Out of the basement: Discovering the value of child care facilities." *Young Children, 1*(15).

*Margie Carter is a college instructor in Seattle who travels widely to speak and consult with early childhood programs. The fifth book she has co-authored with Deb Curtis, **The Art of Awareness: How Observation Can Transform Your Teaching**, released by Redleaf Press in November 2000.*

You Say Staff Deserve Respect? Energize Your Words With Action!

by Karen Stephens

Whether they represent folks in rural areas or big cities, political leaders in the spotlight routinely pronounce children as our nation's greatest resource. And now with hard-core brain research echoing their claim, the "pols" pronounce even louder how vital quality early childhood programs are to our country's welfare. They couch their support in terms of investing in our future workforce, our future bevy of taxpayers. Rarely is it frankly said it's simply the right thing to do.

And so leaders continue to skirt comprehensive measures that would put money behind their rhetoric, behind our children and programs that serve them. You know the economic culture in the United States as well as I do. If one truly believes in something, they back it with greenback. So far, our nation has been mighty measly. We've yet to muster collective commitment to children.

And, by extension, our country has been measly with its early care and education providers. Oh sure, people of note now proclaim child care is a noble calling, not merely babysitting. (How long did it take us to get THAT idea across?!) And they publicly commend early childhood folks for the lasting contribution we make to society. Astute leaders even cite studies that reveal the best path to quality early care and education is to maintain a well educated and trained staff.

But coming through with the resources to compensate quality caregivers — well that idea seems to cool as fast as news camera's spotlights dim. Perhaps positive steps have been made in your program; but on a national scale, the necessity of taking a vow of poverty to work in early childhood still reigns.

So while you and I and our fellow early childhood directors wait for voters to hold leaders accountable for their rhetoric, we're left shouldering the task of maintaining a stable early childhood workforce for American families. You may say I'm being overly dramatic, even pessimistic. I say I'm being realistic.

So how do directors motivate professionals who are usually undercompensated (I'm talking minimum wage even with a four year degree); their skills typically underestimated (Oh,

you're so lucky to sit around and play with kids all day); and their commitment often discounted (So when are you getting a real job?)?

I certainly don't have all the answers. In my 20+ years in early childhood, I've participated in innumerable salary surveys and equity wage initiatives. Some have even come through with meaningful results. But I still rarely see professionally trained early care and education providers paid as well as their public school counterparts.

I'm not naive. Even when better pay becomes a reality, it still takes more than money to motivate and retain well qualified staff. In fact, all things being equal (if that ever happens), intrinsic motivation is far more influential on staff performance and longevity. And the proof is visible in early care and education programs everywhere. Considering the average child care provider makes less than $15,000 annually, I'm not amazed 40% of us leave the early childhood field annually; I'm amazed 60% of us stay in it! Intrinsic motivation is the key.

So, over the years, I've tried to come up with a plethora of tangible ways to help staff feel great about the job they're doing. To feel great in their hearts and minds. I've tried to show respect for their knowledge and to appreciate their talent. And I don't take for granted their dedication to children and families. Some strategies have been simple to carry out; others require more effort. And I must warn you, some may be hokey, but they've all been effective.

I'll share my ideas below. Hopefully, they'll trigger your own imagination. Despite the miles that distance us, together we can work to keep our nation's child care infrastructure — our staff — stable, experienced, motivated, and proud. Until early childhood professionals receive proper monetary compensation, the least we can do is feed their generous spirits with respect and appreciation.

Tangible ways to show staff respect and appreciation

1. Post staff photos near entrance. Include position title, length of service, credentials, and brief biography.

2. Include staff profiles in program newsletters. Distribute newsletters not only to parents and your board but also to program funders and supporters.

3. Include staff in community meetings whenever possible. Introduce them, with title, to *movers and shakers* in attendance. Recognize staff at appropriate events, such as program dedication ceremonies or other public functions.

4. Supply each staff member with a professional business card for networking purposes.

5. Post announcements for parents whenever staff acquire in-service training or renew certificates such as in first aid training.

6. Recommend qualified staff as workshop presenters and training consultants.

7. Send staff's *parents* clippings of program news coverage. (Yes, I'm serious. No matter what your staff's age, they always like to make their parents proud.)

8. Send staff's hometown newspapers press releases, such as announcements of your program's accreditation.

9. Publicly (as well as in evaluations) give staff credit for program improvements. If someone comes up with a creative idea or solution, they should bask in the glory!

10. Organize *regular* events for *team bonding*. Team spirit and camaraderie solidified when we instituted monthly staff dinners. It's a great tradition.

11. Recognize and utilize each staff member's unique talents. I have a teacher with a strong background in physical education. I turn to her for recommendations on new gross motor equipment; she knows I count on her expertise. Another teacher is a wizard with children's computer programs. She's our leader when purchasing decisions are made. AND she gets a subscription to a newsletter on children's software so her input can be well informed. (Meaning, I try — even in small ways — to help her be successful in her job.)

12. Take time to regularly observe in classrooms. At least yearly, *write up* your observations for the room's staff to read within a few days. The speedy feedback is always appreciated. The process is time consuming, but it allows you to document for personnel files as well as to congratulate staff on skillful child guidance or inventive curriculum.

13. Provide one-on-one mentoring when possible. If not, try to find a mentor to fit a staff member's needs. Is a teacher having trouble arranging his environment? Help him with new

arrangements or ask for another staff member's expertise.

14. Encourage staff's hobbies and interests. Is a teacher into bunnies big time? Go ahead and buy a bunny wind sock for her play yard. The kids will learn about wind and she'll appreciate the individualized attention.

15. Make copies of complimentary letters from parents for staff keepsakes.

16. Solicit staff input on decisions that affect them. For instance, they can identify best times to hold parent-teacher conferences.

17. Before preparing supplies and equipment budgets, ask staff to submit a list of recommended purchases.

18. Provide staff with articles, videotapes, or conference information that address topics of special interest. Are teachers interested in learning about the Project Approach? If so, secure funds to send them to a workshop. (My personal dream is to find travel funds so our teachers can visit the Reggio Emilia programs in Italy!)

19. Encourage staff to serve on professional boards and committees. Recognize their efforts when talking to staff, parents, and board members.

20. Compliment staff when they participate in wellness and stress management programs. Literally, they deserve a pat on the back for staying healthy!

21. Recognize staff talent in simple and spontaneous ways. When I go to a conference, I bring something back from the exhibitor's venue. One year, my treasures included a white rabbit puppet that popped out of a magician's black hat. I left the puppet as a surprise on the teachers' desk. An attached note said I marveled at the

magic they do with kids. Yes, it's sappy and sentimental, but the teachers appreciated the thought all the same — and who doesn't need another puppet for the classroom?

22. Provide staff with as much personal space for organization and planning as possible. In days of old, our teachers had lockers, not an office. We've made a bit of progress since then, but not lots. Now four head teachers share a cramped office with one desk, a file cabinet, and a computer. Their office has a love seat for comfort, but also stores our children's library, two refrigerators, and its walls are stacked — literally to the ceiling — with junk supplies creative teachers love to squirrel away. They don't have the separate work stations, staff lounge, or make-it-take-it resource room of their dreams, but they know I'd jump for space that would give it to them.

23. Provide staff time to observe other programs. Mutually decide with staff where they'll observe, why, and when. Arrange for substitutes so staff can leave without burdening those left with the kids.

24. Once a year, take a *fun and interesting* retreat or staff trip together. Visit an outstanding children's museum or go hear a famous children's author speak. Staff will appreciate the time you take to facilitate and organize their enjoyment.

25. Committed caregivers get a lot of enjoyment out of being partners with parents as they nurture children's development. To provide time for the communication the partner requires, bring in extra staff or volunteers at the beginning and ending of the day (that's when parents are most likely to be in the classroom).

26. Bring in a bouquet of wildflowers or a new compact disc to classrooms *just because*. Employees and children respond to aesthetics.

27. Involve staff in any changes in their work environment. We recently renovated one of our site's play yard. I can't tell you how many times I volleyed construction ideas between architects and teaching staff. I continually asked if a proposed design would help or hinder our teachers' job performance. And boy did it pay off! Our program ended up with a much better play yard because the people who used it day in and day out provided guidance. And the staff were pleased to be included in making decisions with other professionals. (In truth, they prevented the committee from making numerous design mistakes!)

28. Serve on committees that organize a community-wide child care provider recognition day. If there isn't one already, start one yourself. Staff will note your efforts to celebrate the important work they do.

29. Teachers love books. Make it a program practice to treat them with birthday or holiday gift certificates to a bookstore. Whether they purchase a book for relaxation or for reading to the children, your program will win either way.

30. Occasionally surprise teachers with helpful supplies that are *tools of the trade*. This could be a big-ticket item, like a laminating machine. But most likely your budget will better afford something simple, like notepads with motivational sayings. "To teach is to touch the future" is a perennial favorite.

31. Encourage and facilitate your program staff and parents' involvement with Worthy Wage Day!

32. Buy each program site a subscription to the newsletter *Rights,*

Raises and Respect — the biannual publication of the National Center for Early Childhood Workforce, $30/year. Send fee to: NCECW, 733 15th Street NW, Suite 1037, Washington, DC 20005-2112.

33. Nominate deserving staff for awards bestowed by the community or profession.

34. Ask staff for recommendations of curriculum books to add to their resource library. (And if they don't have an on-site resource library, create one. Our staff's is located in my office.)

35. Reimburse staff for part or all of their professional dues to organizations, such as local affiliates of the National Association for the Education of Young Children (to identify your local, call (800) 424-2460).

36. Reimburse staff for part or all of continued education costs, whether they be through conferences or college classes. Be sure to recognize staff each time they complete a course that improves their job skills.

So there you are, 36 tangible and specific ways to value your staff and the life affirming work they perform. As you put these ideas into practice, you'll put action behind your hopes and dreams for children. It's the ethical thing to do — the right thing to do. And may the rest of the world follow your lead.

*In 1980, Karen Stephens became director of Illinois State University Child Care Center and instructor in child development for ISU Family and Consumer Sciences Department. She writes the weekly newspaper column, "Keeping the Young at Heart," and is the author of the high school textbook, **The Child Care Professional**.*

Why Do They Stay?
Teachers Make a Career
in the Classroom

by Susan Catapano

Why is there a core group of teachers in every early care and education program who have worked in the field and, many times, at that program for ten or more years? Why do some teachers make a career in the classroom with young children and others move into administration or leave the field?

As the former owner of two early childhood programs, I remember one idyllic period of time when I had a group of dedicated, well-educated, wonderful teachers. That lasted about two years, and I saw them leave one-by-one for very good reasons. Two moved out of state with their new husbands, one left to attend graduate school, one moved into administration, and one completed her student teaching and got a job in the public schools. Yet, there were about three who stayed on and continued the work that all eight had devoted themselves to for the two years they had worked as a team. I comforted myself with the thought that they were self-confident and talented enough to seek out new challenges and that maybe I had helped support them in developing their confidence and talent.

What about the ones who did not leave? They had been in my program soon after I opened, and they were still there many years later after other teachers had moved on. Had I done anything to keep them at the program? Was there something I could do to keep teachers while still supporting their growth and development?

Moving to the university I was able to conduct the research that could answer the questions I pondered when I was a director. In the fall of 2000, I interviewed 31 teachers who had worked in the classroom for ten or more years. These teachers represented seven full day, early care and education programs from a variety of affiliations and corporate organizations: a hospital sponsored program, two not-for-profit programs, a for-profit program, an employer-sponsored program, a school district-sponsored program, and a university lab school. I asked the teachers a series of questions that I thought would lead me to the key to staff retention. The answer that directors everywhere would want to know is: Why do teachers stay in the classroom? I expected to hear that the true key to retention was the leadership skills of the director. My hope was to list those skills so directors everywhere would acquire the skills and be able to retain their staff. We would all live happily ever after.

Retention of good, quality staff is the greatest challenge the director of an early childhood program faces. More challenging than attracting and hiring quality staff, how to keep the good teachers is a constant worry. The reason for the high turnover (38% in 1999), varies with some common themes (NAEYC, 1999). Low wages and limited benefits are usually listed as the top two reasons teachers leave their jobs (CDCA, 1998). Additional reasons teachers leave their jobs are to return to school or to stay home with young children (CDCA, 1998).

I spent approximately 30 minutes with each teacher and asked each one a series of questions. Basic data on the teachers gives a picture of experience, wage, and level of education. Most of the teachers worked with preschool-age children and had been in the classroom ten or more years. The highest level of formal education for most of the teachers was a high school diploma. About half of the teachers (15) reported that they were currently in school, working on a degree. Teachers who had earned an associate's degree stated that they were not going to go on for a higher degree because the program where they worked would not increase their pay for the higher level degree. Teachers earned between $6.50 and $10.50 per hour, with most of the teachers earning $8.50-$9.00 per hour.

When I asked teachers why they stay in the classroom, they all said, "I love the kids!" This could have been the shortest research project in history: "Thirty-one teachers working ten or more years, say that they do it because they love the kids." After the first few gave that answer and then sat and looked at me, I started asking them, "What do you love about them?" That changed the responses dramatically. The teachers squirmed as they tried to put into words why they do what they do everyday. All 31 stated that they enjoyed working with the children, the children made them happy, they loved the children, and the children loved them. Half of the teachers commented that their job and the children were a constant challenge and that challenge kept them interested in teaching.

Several of the teachers became emotional as they described to me what they loved about working with young children. At first, they spoke slowly, as they reflected on this question. It was as though they had never thought about why they chose to work with children. When they began to talk and feel confident in the feelings they were sharing, they spoke for several minutes on what their job really meant to them. Many times they seemed surprised at what they said, questioning what they were saying, then repeating what they had said with conviction.

One teacher described how she had left the field to do something else,

only to return to the classroom within the year. She said that she was really good working with two year olds. She paused, as if to consider what she had said, and then repeated it with force, "Yeah. I'm good at this, I know what to do that will help children." Then she began to cry and apologized for her emotions. She seemed embarrassed and bewildered with what she had said.

One of the teachers called several weeks after I had interviewed her to say that she had thought of something else to tell me. She said that every few weeks she felt as if she were in a state of disequilibrium as she struggled to solve a situation with a child or group of children. The disequilibrium caused her to reflect, think about her practice, search for new information, and question what she was doing and why. The episodes of disequilibrium kept her interested and motivated. She thought that was the reason she had stayed in her classroom for 22 years.

Half of the teachers commented that they understood how children developed and this let them recognize when children were learning from them. I asked them if they had learned child development from a course they took in their degree program or in workshops that they attended. All teachers responded that they had learned child development through a class or workshop; however, they did not fully understand what it all meant until they were able to connect what they had learned to what the children were actually doing. They said this did not happen until they had many years of experience working with children. They recommended that teachers learn child development in a setting that includes children rather than in the usual college classroom or workshop setting. The children help the teachers to make the needed connection from theory to practice.

I also asked the teachers if there was anything about the program where they worked that kept them in the classroom. I thought that the teachers would describe the support and guidance that their director provided to answer this question. Out of the 31 teachers, 26 did talk about the administrative support that they felt at the program where they were currently working. However, a specific administrator or director was not typically discussed as a factor in their job satisfaction. The teachers attributed the administrative support to philosophy and procedures that were administrative policies.

In addition, 23 of the teachers talked about the relationships they had developed with other staff at the program. The word "comfortable" was used by many of the teachers to describe how they felt at the program. They viewed the other teachers and the administration as part of a family, and their role in the family was important to them and the other members of the family. Several talked about how difficult it would be to leave the program; how much they would miss the relationships they had formed with the other staff.

All of the teachers talked about the autonomy they had to make decisions within their classroom. Most of the teachers commented that they had duties outside of the classroom that they performed for the program. One teacher developed the menu and prepared the food order, another teacher kept the art supplies ordered, and another teacher was responsible for keeping the playground safe and the toys available. One of these teachers stated that she felt like the program belonged to her, too. She felt ownership and responsibility to be there. Many of the teachers mentioned the philosophy of the program and the director being compatible with their own philosophy. They commented that this also made them feel comfortable in the program.

As a result of one comment made by a teacher, I added a question to the survey and went back and asked teachers with whom I had already talked with to comment on what kind of early childhood experience they had growing up. Of the 31 teachers interviewed, 28 reported that their families were supportive of them growing up. Twenty-four of the teachers reported that they served in a nurturing role as a child. Many were babysitters for young children and others commented that their home, as a child, was a gathering place for neighborhood children. As young children, these teachers grew up surrounded by adults who had respect for young children. They had learned from their models. It was also interesting that 21 of the teachers came from families of four or more siblings. Two of the teachers came from families with nine children, one came from a family of eleven children, and two of the teachers came from a family of thirteen children. These teachers had grown up in "early care settings"!

As a final question, I asked the teachers where they would be in ten years. They all said they would still be working in the early care and education field. A few were looking forward to retiring and only one hoped to move into an administrative job.

Next steps

What did I find out? Why do teachers make a career in the classroom? It was not the leadership skills of a particular director, because most of these teachers had kept their jobs through several changes of directors at their programs. What should directors do to retain teachers?

Teachers need support.

Teachers clearly rely on the relationships with other staff members within the program. The feeling of being "a family" is important to the teachers who stay in the field and in their programs for long periods of time. Teachers need to feel "comfortable." What that means will be different from program to program; however, it is essential to retaining good teachers. Also, teachers need a supportive organizational structure with a supportive administrator or director.

Although the person was not as important as the structure that was established, the teachers mentioned the need for the director's goals and philosophy to match the teachers' goals and philosophy. Several of the programs where the teachers worked had fairly new directors, within the last three years. Even those teachers talked about having a supportive administration. The longevity of the director is not as crucial as the structure that the director follows. The consistency of policies and procedures were important to the teachers. Knowing what to expect was a key.

Directors should:

1 **Support the development of close relationships among the staff.** Although staff need to develop close, personal relationships with each other, it is important that the administration establish a climate of professionalism and support. Ask staff, "What do you need to feel comfortable in your job?" But keep in mind what Moisey Shopper, a therapist in St. Louis who works with the early care and education community, has cautioned: if the program is organized like a family, then the staff will take on the roles that are typically found within a family. Some of these roles may not be appropriate for the workplace, and directors should not want the role of *mom*. Administrators need to model respectful treatment of each other and of staff. Striking a balance between supporting close

relationships among the staff and maintaining a professional relationship with the organization will be a challenge for the director. The organizational climate that is established within the program will be important for this delicate balance. (See Bloom, P. J., *Blueprint for Action,* for help and guidance on establishing an appropriate and effective organizational climate.)

2 **Establish clear, consistent expectations for teachers.** The program philosophy and the administrator's philosophy must be communicated to everyone working in the program. Teachers should be encouraged to write their own philosophy and hang it in their room and provide copies for parents. In addition, teachers need clear, concise job descriptions that are based on the philosophy of the program and administration. Finally, the evaluation tool used to conduct periodic observations and performance evaluations of the teachers should be based on the job description. In many programs these three things — philosophy, job description, and evaluation, are totally separate. Making them dependent on each other helps keep the expectations for the teachers clear and consistent. Give teachers duties beyond the classroom when teachers are ready for a new challenge.

Teachers recognize child development.

As directors, we have always known that the best teachers could see what children were doing developmentally and why it was important for them to be doing what they were doing. Teachers working in the field for long periods of time recognize developmental milestones that children reach. The teachers said that it took time for them to start recognizing the developmental things that were so important to know.

Directors should:

3 **Help teachers learn about child development.** This is not a new thought or recommendation. We have always known this. However, the theory of child development must be merged with their classroom practice. The best way to do this is through modeling and mentoring rather than formal classes offered in a sterile environment without children. Teachers must be able to discuss why children do what they do, not just describe the action. This reflective thinking takes time, experience, and practice to develop with someone acting as guide. Teachers need opportunities to see examples of development in the children they work with, apply the theory they have learned, and have the mentor scaffold the understanding of the development theory with the teacher. The mentor and the teacher must have time to engage in an open discussion about what was observed and what the developmental implications are.

Teachers grew up in large, supportive families.

When asked about their own childhood, many of the teachers talked about growing up in homes filled with love and about parents or other adults who were there to support their own growth and development. Because the teachers were nurtured, they found themselves in nurturing roles for as long as they could remember. The teachers felt that they had been valued and respected as a child and they then learned to value and respect children.

Directors should:

4 **After seeking legal advice, structure interview questions to discover the early childhood experiences of the applicant.** If you consult with an attorney, you will probably be told not to ask anything of the applicant except name, rank, and social security number. However, that is not realistic in the world of staffing for early care and education programs. With care, questions can be asked that will not violate anyone's rights. Some suggested questions would be:

- Describe some of your early childhood experiences.

- What did you do for fun as a child?

- Who did you enjoy playing with?

- Who nurtured you as a child?

- How did your family view children?

- What is the most important thing you can do for a child?

- Do you still see your childhood friends, or do you still get together with your siblings?

The questions listed above are open-ended and could lead an applicant for a teaching position to discuss some of the key points that the teachers I interviewed mentioned. If the teachers do not answer or seem uncomfortable, move on and that may tell you what you need to know.

These four things for directors to do probably will not solve the retention issue in the early care and education field. They will help directors work to meet the individual needs of the teachers on their staff. We work hard to meet individual needs of families and children, we need to also meet individual needs for teachers. Retention, rather than recruitment, will lead to a quality teaching staff.

References

Bloom, P. J., Sheerer, M., and Britz, J. (1991). *Blueprint for action.* Mt. Rainier, MD: Gryphon House Publishers.

Center for the Child Care Workforce. (1998). *Worthy work, unlivable wages: The national child care staffing study, 1988-1997.* Washington, DC: Center for the Child Care Workforce.

Catapano, S. (1998). *Career development update survey 1998.* St. Louis, MO: Child Day Care Association of St. Louis.

Susan Catapano, Ed.D., is an assistant professor in early childhood education at the University of Missouri in St. Louis. She is the former owner and director of two early care and education programs.

Guidelines for
Effective Use of Feedback

by Roger Neugebauer

One of the most critical challenges facing an early care and education director is improving staff performance. A variety of tools are available to help a director meet this challenge — in-house training, annual appraisals, workshops, conferences, college classes, training films, etc. One of the least glamorous of these tools — providing feedback — is, in fact, the most effective.

With proper feedback, teachers can better control and improve their own performance; without proper feedback, teachers operate blindly, not knowing when their efforts succeed or fail. According to George F. J. Lehner, " . . . feedback helps to make us more aware of what we do and how we do it, thus increasing our ability to modify and change our behavior . . . " (Lehner).

Just how blindly teachers operate without feedback was demonstrated in a study at the University of Michigan (McFadden). Twenty preschool teachers were interviewed about the teaching philosophies and methods. They all expressed attitudes favoring a nonauthoritarian, nondirective approach by the teacher. They preferred to show verbal concern and approval rather than disapproval. This was how they described their teaching. Yet when they were actually observed in the classroom their behavior was quite

different. Observers found their classrooms to be predominantly teacher controlled and teacher centered. Their statements to children characterizing support, approval, or encouragement were fewer than ten percent of their total statements (Schwertfeger). Without feedback teachers may well be operating with false assumptions about the nature of their behavior and its effect on children and parents.

But as anyone who has tried to give advice to a teacher about her teaching style well knows, being effective at giving feedback is not an easy task. The natural tendency is for teachers to become defensive when feedback about their performance is presented. This reaction occurs when the receiver perceives a threat to her position in the organization, to her standing in the group, or to her own self-image.

When individuals become defensive, they are unlikely to accept, or even hear, feedback that is being offered. Instead of focusing on the message, a person reacting defensively " . . . thinks about how he appears to others; how he may be seen more favorably; how he may win, dominate, impress, or escape punishment; and/or how he may avoid or mitigate a perceived or an anticipated attack" (Gibb).

Defensiveness is increased when the receiver perceives feedback to be critical. As Douglas McGregor observes, "The superior usually finds that the effectiveness of the communication is inversely related to the subordinates' need to hear it. The more serious the criticism, the less likely is the subordinate to accept it" (McGregor).

Since teachers need feedback to improve their performance, it is important that a director become skilled at giving feedback that is helpful in a way that does not arouse their defensiveness. The following are recommendations on giving effective feedback:

• Feedback should focus on behavior, not the person. In giving feedback, it is important to focus on what a person does rather than on what the person is. For example, you should say to a teacher "You talked considerably during the staff meeting" rather than "You're a loud-mouth." According to George F. J. Lehner, "When we talk in terms of 'personality traits' it implies inherited constant qualities difficult, if not impossible, to change. Focusing on behavior implies that it is something related to a specific situation that might be changed" (Lehner). It is less threatening to a teacher to hear comments about her behavior than about her traits.

• Feedback should focus on observations, not inferences. Observations are what we can see or hear in the behavior of another person. Inferences are interpretations we make based on what we hear or see (Lehner). Inferences are influenced by the observer's frame of references and attitudes. As such they are much less likely to be accurate and to be acceptable to the person observed. Inferences are much more likely to cause defensiveness.

• Feedback should focus on descriptions, not judgments. In describing an event a director reports an event to a teacher exactly as it occurred. A judgment of this event, however, refers to an evaluation in terms of good or bad, right or wrong, nice or not nice. Feedback which appears evaluative increases defensiveness (Gibb).

It can readily be seen how teachers react defensively to judgments which are negative or critical. But it is often believed that positive judgments — praise — can be very effective as a motivational and learning tool. However, studies have shown that the use of praise has little long-term impact on employees' performance (Baehler). Often praise arouses defensiveness rather than dispelling it. Parents, teachers and supervisors so often "sugarcoat" criticism with praise ("You had a great lesson

today, but . . . ") that "when we are praised, we automatically get ready for the shock, for the reproof" (Farson).

• Feedback should be given unfiltered. There is a tendency for a director to sort through all the observations she makes of a teacher, and all the comments she receives about a teacher, and to pass along that information that she, the director, judges to be important or helpful. This filtering of feedback may diminish its value to the teacher. According to Peter F. Drucker, "People can control and correct performance if given the information, even if neither they nor the supplier of information truly understand what has to be done or how" (Drucker).

• Feedback should be given in small doses. George F. J. Lehner has observed that "to overload a person with feedback is to reduce the possibility that he may use what he receives effectively" (Lehner). Accumulating observations and comments to share with a teacher in periodic large doses may be efficient for the director in terms of time management, but it may make the feedback too voluminous for the teacher to deal with effectively.

• Feedback should be given on a timely basis. If a teacher is given feedback about an incident in her classroom on the day that it occurs, she is much more likely to benefit from this feedback than if it is given to her days or weeks later. When feedback is given close to an event, the recipient is likely to remember all aspects of the event clearly, and thus is able to fit the feedback into a complete picture. When feedback is far removed from the event, the event will be less well remembered and the feedback will make less sense.

An extreme, but not a typical, example of untimely feedback is the annual appraisal. An annual

appraisal is an effort to give feedback about performance over the past 365 days. Not only does this concentrated dose of feedback cause information overload, it also is offered at a time removed from the behavior itself. As such it "is not a particularly effective stimulus to learning" (McGregor). Studies have shown that to be effective, performance appraisals "should be conducted not annually, but on a day-to-day basis" (Levinson).

• Feedback should be given to the teacher as his tool to control his own performance. A teacher is much more likely to benefit from feedback if it is given without strings attached, to use as he sees fit. If a director provides feedback ("The children were restless during circle time today") and then offers advice on how to use it ("I think you should have it earlier in the day"), the teacher is very likely to react defensively over this effort to control his behavior. "The real strength of feedback," according to Drucker, " is clearly that the information is the tool of the worker for measuring and directing himself."

• Avoid giving mixed messages. Through their bodies, eyes, faces, postures, and senses people can communicate a variety of positive or negative attitudes, feelings, and opinions. While providing verbal feedback to a teacher, a director can communicate a conflicting message with her body language. For example, when verbally communicating a nonjudgmental description of a playground scene, a director may be telecasting very disapproving signals to the teacher with the tension in her voice or the expression on her face. When presented with such mixed messages, a teacher invariably elects to accept the nonverbal message as the director's true meaning. As a result feedback gets distorted, and an atmosphere of distrust is created. "Right or wrong, the employee feels that you are purposely hiding something or that you are being less than candid" (Hunsaker).

To avoid communicating mixed messages, you should not give feedback when you are angry, upset, or excited. Wait until you cool down, so that you can keep your emotions under control as you talk. Also you should develop the habit of monitoring your voice tone, facial expressions, and body language whenever you give feedback. Being aware of your body language can help you keep it consistent with your verbal language (Needell).

• Check for reactions. Just as you give feedback, the recipient signals her reaction to it with her body language. You should tune in to these signals as you talk. As Phillip Hunsaker recommends, "Constantly be on the lookout for nonverbal signals that indicate that your line of approach is causing your employees to become uncomfortable and lose interest. When this happens, change your approach and your message accordingly" (Hunsaker).

• Be open to feedback yourself. To develop an effective working relationship, you need feedback from your employees on their reactions to your behavior as much as they need feedback from you. According to organizational psychologist Harry Levinson, "In a superior-subordinate relationship, both parties influence each other, and both have a responsibility for the task." In order to accomplish this task, they must be able to talk freely to each other, and each must have the sense of modifying the other. "Specifically, the subordinate must be permitted to express his feelings about what the superior is doing in the relationship and what the subordinate would like him to do to further the accomplishment of the task" (Levinson).

• Encourage a team approach to feedback. As director, you have a myriad of important tasks in addition to upgrading staff performance. Therefore, it is not possible for you to free up enough time to provide staff members all the feedback they need to improve their performance. In order to provide an ongoing flow of feedback information, you need to enlist all staff members to be feedback givers to each other. First, you must create an atmosphere in your center that encourages staff members to accept responsibility for helping each other improve. Second, you need to train staff members on the proper ways to give feedback. Feedback given in a judgmental, personal, or untimely fashion can be devastating and can poison interpersonal relations. Training can take the form of reviewing the guidelines discussed above in a staff meeting, by doing some role-playing, and by having staff members give each other feedback on how they give feedback. Most of all staff members can learn to be effective feedback givers if you serve as a good model in the way you give feedback.

References

Baehler, J. R. *The New Manager's Guide to Success.* New York: Praeger Publishers.

Drucker, P. F. (1974). *Management: Tasks, Responsibilities, Practices.* New York: Harper and Row, Publishers.

Farson, R. E. (September-October 1963.). "Praise Reappraised." *Harvard Business Review.*

Gibb, J. R. (1971). "Defensive Communications" in David A. Kolb (Editor). *Organizational Psychology: A Book of Readings.* Englewood Cliffs, NJ: Prentice-Hall, Inc.

Hunsaker, P. L., & Alessandra, A. J. (1980). *The Art of Managing People.* Englewood Cliffs, NJ: Prentice-Hall, Inc.

Lehner, G. F. J. (June, 1978). "Aids for Giving and Receiving Feedback." *Exchange.*

Levinson, H. *The Exceptional Executive.* Cambridge: Harvard University Press.

McGregor, D. (1960). *The Human Side of Enterprise.* New York: McGraw-Hill Book Company.

Needell, C. K. (January, 1983). "Learning to Level with Employees." *Supervisory Management.*

Schwertfeger, J. (1972). "Issues in Cooperative Training" in Dennis N. McFadden (Editor). *Planning for Action.* Washington, DC: NAEYC.

Managing From Afar:
Out of Sight, But Not Out of Mind

by Sarah and Robert Boschi, Richard McCool, Sue Portnoy,
and Arlein and Edwin DeGroot

It all used to be so simple. You had just one center. When a teacher was having a problem with a child, you went in and helped her out. When the bus driver called in sick, you drove the bus. When you announced new procedures for serving meals, you were on the spot to remind teachers to follow through. At the time it didn't seem simple at all, of course; but now that you manage centers in five different neighborhoods, you often think longingly of those days when you could work with all your staff on a face to face basis.

Styles of supervision that are effective in single site operations seldom translate well to the management of multiple centers. When you managed a single center, your success rested heavily upon the force of your personality and your attention to endless details. But such traits are not enough when it comes to managing from afar. The force of your personality is diluted when you only see staff members once a week; and trying to attend to all the administrative details of three or more centers would overwhelm even the most extreme workaholic.

Supervising the performance of staff in more than one location requires a unique set of skills. You need to be able to enforce your decisions without your presence, establish rules and procedures without creating a stifling bureaucracy, achieve consistent quality without sacrificing individuality and spontaneity.

In order to experience success in managing from afar, you need to learn how to accomplish results through a system. While the force of your personality will still have an impact, and your attention to details will still be well rewarded, what will make the biggest difference will be your ability to supervise staff through organizational structures and procedures.

What follows are a number of basic guidelines for success in managing staff from afar:

1. Delegate responsibility to someone you can trust.

In a growing organization, one of the hardest things for a director to learn is how to let go. A director who has done everything for years naturally resists giving away responsibility. "Who else can do this as well as I do?" is the typical rationalization. But as demands on her time increase, even the diehard entrepreneur eventually realizes that she can't do it as well as she used to. She needs to lean on others, especially in terms of supervising staff in different locations.

Identifying individuals that you can lean on with confidence must be done with care. You need to find individuals who share your values on working with adults and caring for children, who can take initiative, who can set priorities and stick to them, who can earn the respect and cooperation of the people they supervise, who can be trusted to carry on without close supervision. And most of all, you need to find individuals who you can relate with comfortably on a personal, as well as professional, basis.

What you don't need is a clone of yourself, or a *yes man*. You should not try to find someone who will do everything just like you do, or someone who can be intimidated into doing everything your way. As long as everyone's basic values are in accord, it is healthy for key management staff to follow different paths to accomplishing the same goals. This creates a constructive tension which helps keep you out of a rut and open to new ideas.

2. Develop management talent within your organization.

The best way to find second level managers is to look inside your organization. By promoting from within you can accurately evaluate how you relate to the people on a personal level and how they perform on a day to day basis. When you hire someone from outside, you can never be sure how they will work out in your setting.

You can slowly groom someone from inside by gradually giving him more and more responsibility. If he responds well, you know you've backed a winner. If he flounders, you can try someone else. Some organizations have created an assistant director position at their centers as a means of preparing promising individuals from their teaching staffs for management positions.

3. Turn over responsibility gradually.

Once you have identified a manager, you need to help her grow into the position. One common error is to move too rapidly from where you did everything yourself to where you dump all the responsibility on the new person. A person with a great deal of management potential may fall apart if given too much responsibility at once. You should adhere to the educational maxim that a person grows optimally when presented with moderate challenges which cause her to move just a little bit out of her comfort zone at a time.

By working closely with a new manager at the outset, you will give him the security of learning the ropes without the fear of making some horrendous mistake. Then, by gradually pulling back and leaving him on his own, you will give him the opportunity to build his confidence and develop his own style.

It is healthy for key management staff to follow different paths to accomplishing the same goals.

4. Provide all managers on-going support.

All managers, whether they are new to the job or not, can benefit from continuing support. At Palo Alto/Gerber Centers, for example, it was observed that center directors spent a lot of time on the phone with each other finding out how they handled certain situations, or simply letting off steam. To upgrade the kind of support that was being provided through this informal buddy system, a new position of executive director was created. Experienced directors were promoted to these positions, and each was assigned two or three centers. They call upon their center directors daily and offer whatever kinds of advice or support are needed. Since the executive directors are not formally supervising the center directors, but only offering them support, center directors feel free to admit their mistakes, to ask dumb questions, and to air their complaints without fear of undercutting their credibility in the organization.

Another way to support second level managers is to protect their authority. When a parent comes to you with a problem, or when an old friend from the teaching staff asks for a special

favor, it is tempting just to step in and take care of it as you used to do. But to do so would undermine the authority of your center directors. If staff know that they can make an end run around their center director and get what they want from you, the ability of your center directors to supervise staff will be greatly diminished.

5. Focus everyone's attention and efforts on the basic goals and policies of the organization.

The saying "If you don't know where you're going, you'll never get anywhere" applied particularly well in managing staff from afar. Having clear-cut goals provides a sense of purpose that helps focus the efforts of staff in various locations. You cannot be in every center all the time; but if staff have a clear fix on what they are supposed to accomplish, they can carry on confidently in your absence. If staff do not know what is expected of them, their efforts will be unfocused, inefficient, and often at cross purposes.

It is also critical to communicate to all staff the basic program and personnel policies. If center directors are aware of the organization's policies, they can use these as guides in implementing the day to day program. When issues arise they can use these policies as a basis for decision-making.

If staff know that they can make an end run around their center director and get what they want from you, the ability of your center directors to supervise staff will be greatly diminished.

Communicating the goals and policies of the program to staff in all locations should start during the screening process. An important selection criteria should be that the candidates' teaching, philosophy, and behavior is compatible with the goals of the center. Once hired, teachers should be given an orientation that emphasizes goals and policies. Then throughout the year all staff should be regularly exposed to training that emphasizes techniques for accomplishing these goals and policies.

The goals and policies also need to be reinforced in every way possible. They need to be distributed in writing to all parents and teachers. They should be posted in conspicuous locations in the centers. As head of the organization, you should focus your attention on these when you visit centers or meet with center directors. If you do not give priority attention to the goals and policies, chances are no one else will either.

6. Utilize multiple channels for communication.

When staff are scattered in centers many miles apart, communication can easily fall apart. Yet communication is the glue that holds a program together. To keep morale high and performance improving, all sorts of information, from changes in the goals of the organization to ideas on making play dough, need to be communicated up and down the organization.

To ensure that communication is occurring, an organization should utilize multiple communication channels. The more important a message is, the more ways it should be transmitted. Above all, the more personal the mode of communication the better.

Teaching Centers Inc. holds two meetings a month for the entire staff — one for business and one for training. By making policy announcements in these meetings as opposed to issuing them in writing only, staff

Communicating the goals and policies of the program to staff in all locations should start during the screening process.

are given the opportunity to ask questions about points they don't understand and receive clarification, or point out problems with the proposals that can be discussed.

Weekly meetings with center directors are also a must. These meetings give the head of the organization (or her representative in larger organizations) the opportunity to communicate her current concerns directly. They also give the directors the opportunity to seek advice on unusual problems they are experiencing, and to give notice about any problems which may be looming in the future.

7. Develop a system for controlling center performance.

Once you have entrusted responsibility to dependable people and clearly communicated to them what their goals are, how do you make sure they are following through? Do you tightly monitor all aspects of center operations, or do you put good people in charge and let them do their own thing?

Clearly there needs to be some form of control to ensure that programmatic and financial standards are being complied with. But if controls that you impose are too demanding, you can stifle initiative and undermine morale.

The more important a message is, the more ways it should be transmitted.

To achieve the proper balance in setting up controls, try to impose only those controls which tell you whether or not the program is achieving its goals and complying with basic policies. If your controls indicate that these key

requirements are being met, it should not be necessary to dig any deeper. If they are not being met, then you should take a closer look.

A center director should be able to feel confident that if her center is complying with established goals and policies her performance will be supported. If every decision she makes is second guessed and every aspect of the center's operation is put under a microscope, her motivation to take initiative and exercise responsibility will be diminished. As long as she is meeting her major targets, she should be allowed free reign to operate in a style that is comfortable to her. Overall results should be the criteria of success, not the means of achieving them.

8. Closely monitor key financial indicators.

One area where controls are essential is in terms of bottom line financial figures. Since all centers operate on such a close margin, the financial status of centers needs to be monitored on a regular basis. Money problems need to be caught and addressed early before they escalate to disastrous proportions. This does not mean that every penny earned or spent should be subject to approval by the central office. Once again, controls should focus only on key financial indicators.

A vital report is simply a tabulation of attendance and staffing. This report indicates whether or not a center is in compliance with licensing standards and whether or not the center is overstaffed (i.e., whether or not the center is spending more on salaries than it is taking in on fees). Organizations which experience frequent fluctuations in attendance may find it necessary to require these reports on a weekly or even daily basis. Others, where attendance is more stable, may only review these figures on a monthly basis.

Another key financial control is the monthly income and expense report. This report should be used to spot major discrepancies between what was budgeted for the month and what actually occurred. Unexpected drops in income should be noted, as should major increases in expense items. Such items would then be reviewed with the center director in an informal meeting. Any actions agreed upon in this meeting would then be monitored over the next few months.

9. Maintain frequent site visits.

Out of sight too often is out of mind. There is no better way to keep in touch with what is happening in the centers than to pay them periodic visits. These visits should be handled as informally and supportively as possible. If center directors come to view these visits as inspections, they will become defensive and uptight. As a result, it will not be a productive experience for anyone. Rather, these should be structured as opportunities to clarify policies, to discuss problems and success stories, and to review the needs of the center.

While the major purpose of the visit should not be to check up on the director's performance, you should not miss the opportunity to gather some informal feedback. When you drive up to the center, you may want to put yourself into the perspective of a parent dropping off her child. How does the outside appearance of the facility strike you? Is it well maintained? What about inside?

Does it appear messy, noisy, or downright hazardous?

It may be useful to actually use a checklist of key indicators (one that is written down or one that is kept in your head) for checking to see if the major emphases of your program are being adhered to. Things to observe may include whether the children are engaged in appropriate activities, or whether the teachers are addressing the children appropriately.

One of the hardest things for a director to learn is how to let go.

10. Utilize a variety of tools for assessing program performance.

There are also a number of evaluation approaches that can be employed to check out center performance. The results of these evaluations can be helpful to the central office in its decisionmaking, but they can also be useful to center directors in helping them improve their performance.

Parent satisfaction is a key indicator of performance and needs to be regularly evaluated. Educo Schools send out a two page evaluation form to every parent every year. By offering rewards to the classrooms that have the most questionnaires returned, Educo has managed to achieve an 80 percent rate of return. These questionnaires provide valuable feedback on how the program is perceived by the parents.

Another means of measuring parent perceptions is to interview all parents

Try to impose only those controls which tell you whether or not the program is achieving its goals and complying with basic policies.

who withdraw from the program. While parents may be reluctant to fully discuss their reasons for departing with the center director, they do tend to be more open with someone higher up in the hierarchy. Again this information can be useful both to the central office and to the center director.

To get a fix on the staff perspective, Teaching Centers Inc. holds monthly teacher advisory committee meetings. One teacher from each center as well as representatives from the central office attend this meeting. Organization-wide issues that are on teachers' minds — problems, questions, suggestions — are discussed. (Problems that are unique to a particular center are reserved for discussion with the center director.) Minutes are kept, and every employee receives a copy of these minutes with their next paycheck. This forum helps to keep the central office staff in touch with emerging issues among the employees. It also helps the teachers feel more a part of the organization as a whole, and lets them know that their feelings and opinions are treated seriously.

Sarah and Robert Boschi are owners of Teaching Centers, Inc. in Wauwatosa, Wisconsin. Richard McCool is president of Educo, Inc. in Vienna, Virginia. Sue Portnoy is a regional manager of Palo Alto Preschools/Gerber Children's Centers, stationed in Scottsdale, Arizona. Arlein and Edward DeGroot are owners of Amrein's Child Development Centers in metropolitan Dallas, Texas.

Helping Employees Cope With Change

by Lorraine Schrag, Elyssa Nelson, and Tedi Siminowsky

• *In response to community demand, the ABC Child Care Center opened a room for infants. The new program was an instant success and soon had a waiting list. However, staff in the preschool room were less than excited. The director spent so much time in setting up the new room that she barely had time to help the rest of the staff with their problems. In addition, budgets for classroom supplies were cut to the bone in order to equip the new room.*

• *The head teacher in the four year old room quit after ten years of teaching at Happy Days Nursery School and was replaced by a new teacher. The rest of the teachers were upset that they were not considered for promotion and were threatened by the new teacher who arrived with lots of enthusiasm and new ideas.*

• *The arrival of the computers was greeted with delight by the children and with despair by the teachers at the Elm Street After School Program. The teachers were intimidated by the computers and were afraid that their rapport with the children would disappear in a rush of arcade fever.*

These are three typical examples of change and its impact on staff in child care centers. We teach children in our centers to be flexible, open, and creative. But when change occurs at the center, we often find that it is the adults who are the most inflexible and the most resistant to change. This resistance may manifest itself in anger, anxiety, bitterness, or despair.

Staff members who are unable to adapt to changes in their work environment may react by complaining to their co-workers, thus chipping away at staff morale. They may vent their frustration by refusing to go along with the change. Their anxiety or anger may cause them to perform below their ability. Or they may just quit, or perform so poorly that they end up being fired.

As a director you would like to avoid these reactions to change, but you know that you cannot avoid making changes. Whether your program is an expanding multi-site system or a small, stable nursery school, you will inevitably be introducing some magnitude of change into your organization. So the question is *how can you introduce change without upsetting your staff?*

The following are five suggestions on helping staff cope with change. They deal with ways to select and develop change-oriented staff members, and they offer some nonthreatening ways to introduce change. But implicit in all of them is the message from director to staff, "I value you so much that I'm going to do whatever I can to bring you along with this change."

#1. Building a resilient staff

The most direct way to minimize staff resistance to change is to build a staff that looks upon change as a challenge rather than as a threat. This involves not only including openness to change as a criteria in the selection process but also using staff development opportunities to strengthen the commitment of staff members.

Openness to change is not, of course, a trait that can be readily measured during the selection process. But there are some fairly reliable indicators to watch for. For example, it may be helpful to get candidates talking about what they did and didn't like about their previous jobs. If dealing with changes comes up in the negative category, this may be a meaningful clue as to what to expect. Also, candidates who are free flowing in their thinking, and who have many ideas to talk about other than that they really love kids, are likely to be able to deal well with change.

Exposing candidates to even a small deviation from the norm in the selection process can also demonstrate how they deal with change. For example, having candidates participate in a group interview as opposed to the expected one-on-one interview can show how they handle the stress of the unexpected.

It is important, once a teacher is hired, to carefully observe her during her probationary period to see how she handles change in practice. Observe how well she deals with small changes, such as being asked to change rooms to fill in for absent teachers. Another factor to observe is how comfortable new teachers are in discussing the problems and successes they are experiencing. Openness in discussing such issues is a positive indication that a person is open to change.

On an ongoing basis, any staff development efforts that get staff members more committed to the goals of the organization are likely to yield positive benefits in times of change. The more that staff members believe they are an integral part of the team, the more willing they will be to put up with any discomforts brought on by changes. Staff, on the other hand, who have little commitment to the organization, who are just along for the ride, will react strongly to any inconvenience or stress.

#2. Avoiding leadership blind spots

When the director of the Elm Street After School Program decided to buy computers for her program, she was sure the idea would succeed. She had researched the educational implications of computers; she had read hundreds of software reviews to be sure she selected programs that were truly educational as well as entertaining; and she tried these programs out on the computers she planned to buy to make sure everything worked as described. She even prepared carefully for breaking the news to the staff by pulling together the statistics and research to bolster her case.

When the teachers greeted her presentation with misgivings, she set up a computer and, with great enthusiasm, showed them two of the programs in action. Two weeks later, with the computers gathering dust on the shelves, the director wondered what had gone wrong — why had the staff opposed her great idea?

What went wrong was that the director had blind spots which prevented her from seeing what was happening. She was so preoccupied with launching *her baby* that she became oblivious to what was bothering the teachers. When teachers showed signs of resistance, the director responded by rolling out more artillery to win them over to her side. Instead, she should have tried to understand their concerns, to see what was happening from their point of view.

More often than not, when teachers resist a new idea they are not so much opposed to the idea itself as they are anxious about the social consequences of the change. They may be concerned with how this change will affect their relationship with the children, whether it will keep them from working closely with teachers they enjoy, whether it will force them outside their comfort zone to work in an area where they lack expertise.

If the director is so preoccupied with the logistics of implementing the change that she fails to see such social and emotional impacts of change, no amount of haranguing on the merits of the idea will overcome teachers' resistance. When signs of resistance appear, the director may find it helpful to talk to concerned staff members on a one-to-one basis to explore their feelings about the change. An alternative is to pull aside teachers who have already bought into the change and ask for their views on what it is that is causing some staff members to fight the idea. Only when the director has overcome her blind spots and seen the root causes of resistance can she begin to work toward successful implementation of the change.

#3. Keeping staff informed

A large measure of the anxiety aroused during a period of change is caused by fear of the unknown. If a director decides to add an infant component and only announces this in a cursory way, staff members may well be consumed with a host of uncertainties: Will teachers be taken from our classrooms to staff the new program? Will this new program receive top priority for any new money for equipment? Will salary increases be put on hold while the new program is getting started?

Most of this anxiety can be dissolved by keeping staff informed both before and after the change. There may well be a temptation to withhold disclosing a plan until it is finalized, with the reasoning that there is no need to get staff all worked up ahead of time. However, more often than not, inklings of this plan will have leaked through the grapevine anyway. Rather than letting these rumors build erroneous fears, it is usually best to keep staff up to speed from the start on developments that will affect them.

When informing staff about an impending change, it is best to fill them in on the big picture. Let them know what has prompted you to think about making the change; how this change fits in with your center's current goals, or how and why you are shifting your goals; and what the advantages and disadvantages are to making the change.

Then, viewing the change from their perspective, describe how you antici-pate this change will impact the day-to-day operations of the center and how it will impact them personally. Try to be as candid as possible in addressing any concerns people might have. If there may be some negative or unpredictable conse-quences, don't try to gloss over or conceal these. When staff find out later that you were less than honest with them, your credibility will be damaged, if not destroyed.

Sometimes it would appear that a new idea or a change in plans or policies is too complex to fully explain to all staff members. When economic pressures force a center to increase enrollment in the preschool rooms from 18 to 20, a detailed bud-getary discussion of all the factors and alternatives may well be beyond the grasp of staff members who aren't versed in accounting. So the director may be tempted to say simply, "We need to do this for budgetary reasons — trust me!" If staff members are being forced by this change to work harder for the same pay, they may view this expla-nation by the director as somewhat

---

Who Can Cope with Change?

Some people have the ability to adapt to change, others do not. Larry Wilson, head of the Wilson Learning Corporation, has identified five attitudes shared by those who are best able to deal with change. If your center is likely to experience considerable change, you may want to keep these attitudes in mind as you select and develop your staff:

- **Challenge** — an openness to change. People possessed with this mindset view change as an opportunity, rather than as a threat.

- **Commitment** — a high degree of involvement in what one is doing. A staff member who believes in what the organization is doing, who is committed to the goals of the organization, is likely to be supportive of changes that improve the performance of the organization.

- **Control** — a sense of personal impact on external change. If staff members, through their ongoing relationship with the organization, feel as if they are not powerless in the face of change, that they will be able to influence the course of change, they will be more accepting of change when it occurs.

- **Confidence** — the recognition that no situation puts your personal worth on the line. Confident people are comfortable with who they are, with their faults as well as their strengths, and with others. They tend not to read into activities (such as organizational changes) implications about their worth. They are less inclined to avoid things that they may not do well, and they are more willing to take risks.

- **Connection** — the extent of interpenetration you are willing to estab-lish between yourself, others, and your environment. Interaction with the external environment, or making connections, somehow appears to allow a parallel process to take place internally, enabling a person to develop an increasingly sophisticated system of adaptability to change.

---

less than satisfactory. While the director should not try to razzle dazzle the teachers with fancy charts and figures, she should take the time and trouble to translate the reasons into terms that all staff members can understand.

Helping staff fully understand change is not simply an act of profes-sional courtesy. In general, it is in the best interests of the program to have teachers who understand what they are doing. A person who does not fully comprehend what she is doing will not be a fully productive worker.

She will not be able to exercise informed and intelligent judgment on what she is doing. If the after school teachers do not really under-stand how the computer programs the kids are using work, they will be handicapped in their efforts to help the children learn through computers.

#4. Involving staff in the change process

An even better way to bring staff along with a change is to have them participate in the process of change.

There are two advantages to inviting participation. First, staff who are involved in planning a change have an ego investment in seeing that it succeeds. They will work hard to make their plan work. Second, by including staff in the planning process, you are multiplying the size of your solution pool. By having more minds focused on solving a problem, particularly minds of people whose work is central to the purpose of the organization, the chances of arriving at a successful conclusion are increased dramatically.

However, for participation to be effective, it must be true participation and not just a gimmick. Including teachers from the preschool room on a committee to plan the new infant room does not constitute participation if the director has already drafted the plans and just wants a rubber stamp approval. Asking for teachers' opinions on the new staffing structure in a staff meeting is not true participation if the director doesn't intend to take seriously what they have to say. Participation only works if those asked to participate feel like they are participating and not simply playing a game.

There are myriad ways to get people involved in the change process. One common way is to appoint staff members to serve on a task force. If a new head teacher is being selected, having other teachers participate on the screening committee can be very helpful. Having the support and agreement of the teachers who will be working with the new teacher minimizes feelings of resentment and promotes teamwork.

In other instances, however, appointing a committee is a poor excuse for participation. Unless they are given a very specific, achievable charge, committees often become cumbersome and indecisive. When confronted with a thorny problem, a director

may achieve the best results by picking staff members' brains on a one-to-one basis or by conducting brainstorming sessions at regular staff meetings.

Other informal types of participation can have valuable results. If a new head teacher is coming in, you can team her up with one or two of the more experienced teachers and ask them to teach her the ropes.

If you are moving to a new space, you can take field trips to the new space ahead of time so that teachers can start planning how to use it.

If you are adding an infant component, you can assign different staff members to be in charge of selecting equipment, buying books and materials, and designing the space.

#5. Providing support

During a period of change, when staff members typically are most anxious or angry, the director is often the most distracted and, therefore, least available to relieve this tension. An integral part of the process of planning for change should be thinking through how extra support will be provided to staff during this period.

The most basic form of support that can be provided is to publicly acknowledge at the outset that staff members are likely to feel anxious, ignored, angry, or disoriented. Let them know that such feelings do not reflect a weakness on their part, but that they are an inevitable result of a turbulent, uncertain period. Assure them that someone will be available to listen to their concerns, to answer their questions, and to help them in any way they need to survive this traumatic period.

To underline your support, you should strive to maintain, even to increase if necessary, the frequency of staff meetings. You should schedule

specific times when staff members know that they can talk to you on a one-to-one basis. If you disappear from the face of the earth, and if standard communication forums are cut off during this period, staff will have limited productive means of expressing their feelings.

You may also need staff members to take on increased responsibilities as you may be distracted and unable to be as involved in the day-to-day operation of the program. If you see this happening, you should not let it occur by default. To avoid feelings of resentment, let staff members know ahead of time that they are being entrusted with increased responsibilities. Let them know that you are available if they have serious concerns, but that basically you expect them to act independently, and that you trust they can succeed. Then let them go. Don't be a Monday morning quarterback, second guessing all of their decisions. This is not the time to be hypercritical.

You will inevitably find that, having lain all the above groundwork, there will still be some individuals who will need even more direct support. Most individuals do want to deal successfully with change — it's all a part of growing up. As much as they may overtly resist change, there is a spot in them that wants to grow. What you need to do is to go for that spot, to find a way to get them excited about some aspect of what is going on. Encourage them to take that risk, and let them know that you are supporting them all the way.

If you can't get a teacher to work with the computers in the classroom, maybe you could get her to take a computer home to mess around with over the weekend. If you can't convince the cook that the new menu is a good idea, maybe you could get her to cooperate if you were able to work a kitchen aide into the budget.

Unfortunately, you will not be able to find that spot with all people. There will be some people who will not be able to deal with change no matter how much preparation and support you provide. They may not give you much feedback about how they are feeling or why they are having a hard time. They won't provide you with anything to hook onto to turn them around. Or they may be passive resisters — they may agree with everything you say but then go out and perform as they always have, totally disregarding the changed expectations.

Before investing too much time, you need to decide whether it would be in the best interests of the program to keep trying to turn these individuals around or to let them go. Sometimes those who are having a hard time with change will recognize that the stress is too much for them, and they will select themselves out of early childhood. Others will lack such self-insight and will need to be told that both in the interest of the program and of their career they are being asked to leave.

Throughout the process of change, your attitude as the leader in the organization is critical. If you approach change with enthusiasm and confidence, this spirit can infect your staff. If you maintain your focus on the goals of the organization throughout a period of change, people will not lose sight of the ultimate purpose of change. If you view your role during change as being a facilitator — one who carefully prepares the way, who keeps channels of communication open, who provides support wherever it is needed — you will make the change easier for everyone. If you respect your employees, you will take the time and effort to bring them along.

Chapter 5

Overcoming Challenging Situations

Moving Staff Through Difficult Issues

by Margie Carter and Ann Pelo

As I travel the country, there are some common themes that come up in most of the seminars I facilitate for directors: What do you do about teachers who seem unmotivated to see themselves as professionals or take any initiative to improve aspects of their room or the program as a whole? Why is so much of my time spent with conflicts among our teachers? How can I keep my dedicated teachers from becoming so discouraged by the staff turnover we have to face every year? These are weighty issues, not likely to be solved by some one minute manager technique. I think they are fundamentally tied to the kind of leadership that exists in a program and the organizational climate that is created and maintained.

I'd like to share some examples of how one program I've worked with over a number of years has worked through some of these difficult questions. The staff at Hilltop Children's Center in Seattle, Washington, would be the first to tell you there is no such thing as resolving these issues once and for all. Instead, what is needed is an understanding of the dynamics at play, the context from which these issues typically emerge, and a steady disposition and process to continually move through them. Consciously mentoring an expanding leadership team is another important ingredient that has helped Hilltop get through the reoccurring difficulties that

seem to come with the early childhood territory.

The examples listed come from paying attention to these ingredients, with Ann Pelo a long time teacher in the program, stepping forward to assist the director and assume a more active leadership role beyond her classroom. She developed some of these strategies in consultation with me, but refined and carried them out with remarkable skill and results. I'm encouraging Ann to do further writing so that others can benefit from these Hilltop stories. For now, here are some sound bites of their experiences which might get your own creative juices flowing.

Staff with differing levels of commitment

Hilltop is a small, non profit, accredited full-time early childhood program serving about 75 three to nine year olds with a teaching staff of 16. A core of teachers has been there between five and 25 years, while others come and go each year. Over the years they have held firm to the notion of having all staff designated as *co-teachers* working with a shared vision and sense of purpose for the program, with no hierarchy in teacher titles or job descriptions. This strongly held value continually bumped up against the reality of some staff taking on more responsibilities than others, with some viewing this work as a life-long commitment, while others limit their involvement for a variety of reasons. Expanding paid planning time for teachers was a significant accomplishment for Hilltop, but it brought these contradictions to a head as some teachers used this time, and many more unpaid hours, to plan, work with documentation, and partner with families, while others did little of this type of work. The myth that everyone was carrying equal responsibilities was exposed, with the acknowledgement that it was fomenting a mixture of resentment and guilt. The question became urgent: how do we rectify this situation while continuing to value and celebrate the contribution of each staff member, even as those contributions look quite different?

Strategy:
Getting clear about what the vision involves

Steady discussion about the need for a change in structure led to an all staff retreat held one Saturday. It began with each staff person getting a large paper with a picture of the human heart. Each was asked to write on one side what breaks their hearts or makes their hearts ache, and on the other side, what lifts their hearts and makes them soar. The discussion flowing from this got the frustrations and the joys on the table and set the stage for an amiable restructuring process.

Next the staff worked in small groups to create a list of all the work involved in making a classroom work well. This included everything from watering plants to meeting with families and co-workers, to daily observations and documentation for curriculum planning. For some, this was an eye-opening staff-development process as they discovered all the invisible, behind the scenes work of being a teacher.

As a group they then coded the list to designate which tasks needed to be done by everyone and which could be done by just some people. Three small groups then fleshed out a different possible structure which could incorporate all the responsibilities and allow for differing levels of commitment and allocations of paid time away from the children. The one that was ultimately embraced by everyone was a concentric ring model with a core of responsibilities that everyone would assume in the center, and additional responsibilities

for each ring further out from the center.

Strategy:
Finding your place in the circle

In the next few months Ann and her director, Susie Eisman, worked to refine the model and develop a self-assessment tool for each staff member to use to determine where they saw themselves on the circle of concentric rings. These self-assessments became the focus of individual meetings with the director to choose a ring that fit individual goals, strengths, and commitments. Each room team met to review everyone on that team's decision to determine if all responsibilities were covered for that room; assignments were then formalized. Teachers on Ring 4 became the leadership team with more release time for their responsibilities and meeting together with the director. In the succeeding months, people eased into the new structure with fewer tensions and more clarity about responsibilities and leadership.

Staff communications and conflicts

You can usually get a quick weather report on a program's organizational climate by taking a look at staff communications and how conflicts are handled. Does it feel mostly sunny, partly cloudy, or always stormy? At Hilltop, with its articulated vision of being a caring, learning community, people were reluctant to bring up disagreements or engage in conflicts. No one wanted to hurt anyone's feelings or make them feel isolated or left out. Neither did they want to challenge co-workers' behaviors, even though some undermined the collective good.

Fortunately, nearly all of the Hilltop staff is skilled at building strong

relationships with the children and helping them work through conflicts. This is a strength Ann and I felt could be built on to help staff develop more authentic relationships with each other. Ann facilitated a series of meetings which brought the staff closer together and resulted in a written set of agreements entitled, "Strengthening Our Relationships: A Statement of Values and Principles for Navigating Conflict and Challenge."

Strategy:
Knowing what's true about you

With the aim of being playful and reflective, the staff was first asked to introduce themselves with a childhood message about conflict. Described more fully in *Training Teachers: A Harvest of Theory and Practice* (Carter & Curtis, 1994, Redleaf Press), this activity involves asking people to get up and walk around the room introducing themselves by repeating to each other their name and a phrase that captures what they learned as a child about how to view conflict. The debriefing discussion led to new self-insights and awareness of the *whys behind* their differing approaches to conflict.

This discussion was followed by a four-corners activity, also described in *Training Teachers*, in which people were given four choices of possible ways they might be approaching conflicts and asked to discuss those with others. For example, when it comes to handling conflict now in my life I am like a German Shepherd, an ostrich, a giraffe, a parrot. When there's a conflict I react most negatively to, I_____ ; With practice, I hope to handle conflict like

_____ .

During this meeting people were able to light-heartedly look at themselves and each other's relationship to conflict and find themselves intrigued, rather than fearful, eager, rather than evasive or defensive. Examples of what came up during this meeting were playfully referred to in the following weeks, along with some deeper thinking.

Teachers were eager to read the handout given to them, "Collaboration, Conflict, and Change: Thoughts on Education as Provocation." (Jones & Nimmo, *Young Children*, January 1999). A meeting the following month went further with these activities to explore family of origin theories with regard to how we approach conflict. The discussion points from the activities began to form the initial ideas for a statement of values and principles.

Strategy: Representing ourselves with symbols

Because Hilltop values all learning styles and symbolic languages, not just those that are verbal linguistic, Ann used part of one meeting to have all staff members create a symbol for themselves about what they were discovering or affirming about their relationship to conflict. There were a variety of art materials available, soft music, and lighting. The symbolic representations were brought to a candle lit table and created a powerful collective picture. There were more activities, a discussion of the handout from the previous month, and finally, some work on a collective statement about how they wanted to navigate conflict together. The group did their evaluations of the meeting while listening to Bela Fleck's song, "Communication is the only way, start saying what you mean today."

The impact of turnover

After such an important year of drawing closer together, successfully restructuring staff positions, and working on written agreements about communications and navigating conflict, it was particularly devastating for the staff to learn about two resignations among their ranks. It was tempting to want to just cheerlead and brush this news aside with best wishes for the departing staff, but Ann and her director recognized this staff turnover had the potential to demoralize everyone and undermine much of what they had accomplished over the year. Because this news came just four weeks before *Worthy Wage Day*, they seized the moments and Ann designed some strategies for them to acknowledge their feelings and fuel their desire to re-engage with the *Worthy Wage Campaign*.

Strategy: Pass the basket

Ann gave each staff person a pen and multiple pieces of paper. They were asked to identify the specific ways in which the early childhood staffing crisis was impacting them, writing each on a separate piece of paper and putting it in the basket provided. The basket was then passed around; and, one by one, people read each of the papers. This created a powerful picture of what they were experiencing and brought these feelings out of isolation and into collective action.

Strategy: Collaborate with parents in advocacy efforts

Sharing the sadness and setbacks of staff turnover with Hilltop families felt important, so they could use this opportunity to fuel some collaborative activism. In the face of continual news of budget cuts and the economic mandate of fighting terrorism, parents and teachers alike are feeling an even greater pinch. At their *pass the basket* staff meeting focused on the staffing crisis, Hilltop teachers decided to set aside three afternoons, from 4:30-6:30, leading up to *Worthy Wage Day*, to invite families to join them in creating a collaborative mural which would express their understandings of the problem and their proposals for public policy action.

They would invite the local media to attend and give them press packets about the crisis developed by the Center for the Child Care Workforce (CCW) for *Worthy Wage Day*. Documentation of this mural making and written materials about the staffing crisis will now be woven into orientation packets for new families, educating and inviting them to become ongoing Worthy Wage activists until the early childhood staffing crisis is resolved.

Difficult issues abound in early care and education programs. But when the director expands her leadership team toward a bigger vision, and the organizational climate keeps staff learning and growing closer, these issues don't hold the program back. In fact, many programs grow stronger when they discover they can move through even the toughest of times.

Margie Carter has worked as a staff trainer at Hilltop Children's Center where Ann Pelo has taught for ten years. Ann is featured in the videos, "Children at the Center," "Setting Sail," and "Thinking Big." She has co-authored a book entitled That's Not Fair: A Teacher's Guide to Activism with Young Children. Ann is particularly interested in anti-bias and peace education and in the philosophy of the schools of Reggio Emilia, Italy. Margie lives in Seattle where she teaches at Pacific Oaks College NW. She travels widely to speak and consult with early childhood programs. She is co-authoring a new book on environments with Deb Curtis. Contact Margie through her web site with Deb Curtis at www.ecetrainers.com. You can reach Ann at www.hilltopchildrenscenter.com.

When Friction Flares — Dealing With Staff Conflict

by Roger Neuebauer

"Aside from the harm an uncontrolled conflict does to an organization, your inability as manager to control it may lead to your overthrow, either by angry contestants or by impatient bystanders."
— Theodore Caplow

"Your job in resolving personality conflicts between your subordinates is to make the person involved in the conflict aware how his or her behavior is adversely affecting others, and how it is thereby adversely affecting the operation."
— Thomas L. Quick

"It is not best that we should all think alike; it is difference of opinion which makes horse races."
— Mark Twain

These are the times that try directors' souls — when arguments erupt over the cleanup of shared space, when staff meetings turn into acrimonious debates over lousy working conditions, when two teachers every day find new pretexts to prolong their personal feud.

Wouldn't it be wonderful if you could wave a magic wand and all this disharmony would disappear? Unfortunately, in a demanding, interaction-intensive profession such as early care and education, where pressures and feelings run high, conflict is inevitable.

There is no way a director can, or even should, drive all conflict out of the life of the center. The challenge is how to manage dissension so that it contributes to the growth, and not the deterioration, of the organization. The following are some guidelines for accomplishing this.

Encourage healthy conflict

Asking a center director to foster conflict is like asking a yuppie to shop at K-Mart. However, in a creative organization, the clash of ideas and opinions keeps the organization growing and improving. In a creative organization, the types of healthy conflict described in the "Signs of Healthy Conflict" box happen all the time.

As a leader in your organization, there are a number of steps you can take to promote healthy conflict:

● **Don't let your ego run amuck**

I recently participated on a committee of teachers and board members tussling with the growing need for infant care. For months we hotly debated whether the center should offer infant care, where we could locate it, and how much we would have to charge to provide a high quality program. When we presented our recommendations to the full board, a lively discussion ensued. Finally, the director took the floor and stated that she didn't believe children that young should be in a center. After her statement, the discussion sort of petered out until finally a motion was made and passed to table the recommendations indefinitely.

This director had no intention of throwing a wet blanket on the debate — she assumed she simply was expressing her views as one member of the board. What she failed to take into account was that the opinion of the leader of any organization is packed with positional power. As a leader, unless you work hard to undermine your authority by behaving like a fool, your opinions may exert an overwhelming influence on discussions.

If you want your staff to express their opinions, be it in meetings or in one-to-one discussions, you must exercise discretion in expressing your own opinions. This is not easy.

Most directors I have met over the years tend to be take charge people. They care deeply about the success of their centers and take it personally when things go wrong. Their egos are heavily invested in their work, and they like to have things done their way.

Take charge directors often do unintentionally put a damper on the clash of ideas in their centers by jumping in with a position on every issue. Particularly if a director has strong verbal skills, she can easily dominate any discussion.

If you value the expertise and insights of your staff members, you need to keep your ego in check. Resist that very natural urge to voice your opinion on anything and everything — at least until everyone else has had their say.

• Beware the peacemaker

Often within families there is an unspoken rule that one should not express angry feelings. On the surface this creates a placid appearance. But the result is that anger continues and festers, potentially causing long term emotional difficulties for family members.

The same scenario can play itself out in organizations. When emotions erupt at the center, a peacemaker (maybe the director, maybe not) will rush in and urge everyone to calm down and keep their angry

feelings in check. Once again, this may still the waters, but it often leaves conflicts unresolved. Suppressed anger can eat away at staff morale and, if allowed to intensify, can result in an even greater explosion later on.

A wiser, though often less pleasant, course for a director to take is to foster an environment where the true expression of emotions is tolerated. In the long run this results in a better working climate because conflict can be brought out in the open where it can be dealt with and resolved.

On the other hand, you don't want to create a haven for hotheads and chronic complainers. You need to follow three basic rules in dealing with expressions of anger . . .

First, don't answer anger with anger. If you respond to anger in kind, emotions can quickly escalate out of control.

Second, listen. When a staff member is letting off steam, don't interrupt, argue, or explain. Let them get the feelings out of their system as much as possible before you intervene.

Third, ask questions. To move a discussion toward a constructive stage, ask specific questions to clarify the cause of the problem and then start the exploration of solutions.

• Don't take it personally

You want to create an atmosphere in your center where all staff members feel free to voice questions, concerns, and objections — where healthy conflict flourishes. You want your staff members to be confident that they can confront you openly over organizational issues and not worry that you will hold this against them.

You can, of course, tell people that you welcome their critical comments, and write them memos assuring them that this is true. But the bottom line is that people won't believe this until you demonstrate your tolerance in real life.

In part, this requires a significant sell job on yourself. You must believe that you and your center will benefit from the clash of ideas and opinions. When a debate flares over teaching practices, the use of common space, the center's ratios, or other program issues, you must truly view this debate as an opportunity to improve the program. If you are not comfortable with conflict and criticism, your body language will surely send out warning signals to staff members that their comments are not being well received.

You can also demonstrate that you welcome open discussions by rewarding people who take risks by saying what they think. At the end of a heated, maybe even emotional,

---

Signs of Healthy Conflict

Conflict among staff in a center can be constructive if it . . .

- generates new ideas, new perspectives
- provokes an evaluation of organizational structures or center design
- brings individuals' reservations and objections out into the open
- heightens the debate about pending decisions or problems
- forces the reexamination of current goals, policies, or practices
- focuses attention on problems inhibiting performance at the center
- energizes staff — gets them actively involved in the life of the center

debate in a staff meeting, acknowledge that the discussion may have put many participants under stress, that you appreciate everyone's honesty and openness, and that you believe that the program will be the better for having dealt with the issues at hand.

If individual staff members appear to be particularly upset by a confrontation, take pains to reassure them in private that you bear no grudge toward those who disagree with you. Thank them for expressing their views. Smile and behave normally towards them.

Discourage unhealthy conflict

Not all conflict is positive. A dispute over an organizational issue which is ignored by the director can deteriorate into acrimony and bring down staff morale. A personal feud which erupts between two or more staff members can distract participants from doing their jobs.

One important challenge for any director is to distinguish between healthy and unhealthy conflict. When conflict exhibits manifestations such as those listed in the "Signs of Unhealthy Conflict" box, you need to intervene.

• Don't allow conflicts to escalate

Often it is tempting to ignore a minor flare up among staff members and hope that it will fade away. Sometimes this may work, but more often than not the "hands off" approach backfires.

An outbreak of hostility can eat away at staff morale and productivity. The longer you allow it to rage out of control, the more likely your credibility as a leader will be undermined as well. You must act quickly to contain damaging conflict. It is

---

Signs of Unhealthy Conflict

Conflict among staff in a center can be destructive if . . .

• one person or faction is bound and determined to emerge victorious
• focus of the debate changes but the adversaries remain the same
• discussion never moves from complaints to solutions
• staff members start taking sides
• parents or other outside parties get drawn into the debate
• continuing acrimony starts to erode staff morale
• dissension continues even after a decision is hammered out
• debate focuses on personalities, not issues

---

especially helpful to intervene before a private feud has boiled over into a public feud. Once positions have been taken in public, it will be harder to get disputants to back down for fear of losing face.

• Be a mediator, not a judge

When faced with a conflict among staff members, you may quickly develop an opinion about who is right and who is wrong. Your temptation will be to end the dispute immediately by playing the role of the judge and declaring a winner. More often than not, you end up being the loser in this case, no matter how wise your decision. The winners believe they were right all along, and therefore owe you no thanks; and the losers end up bitter because you made a stupid or biased decision.

You are better off in the long run to play the role of an impartial mediator working with both parties to hammer out a compromise that all can support. In this case, both parties feel they had a hand in shaping the outcome and will be more committed to making it work.

• Match your response to the severity of the conflict

In the case of a minor squabble between two or more staff members, you may find it sufficient to commu-

nicate to the individuals involved that you recognize that a problem exists and that you expect them to work out a resolution themselves. Give them a deadline; check back to make sure they followed through.

If the individuals can't work out their own problem, you may need to bring them together in your office and force them to confront the issues causing the conflict. Ask each individual to state their perception of the problem and then their suggestions for a solution. Your role is to lead them to agree on a solution.

In some cases such a face-to-face thrashing out of the issues may work. When emotions are running high, however, a confrontation may actually escalate the conflict. When one angry staff member confronts another in your presence, this may cause both parties to intensify their feelings. In order to save face, they may harden their positions.

In this case, you may need to play more of the role of a third party intermediary. Interview each party to the conflict in private and ask them to explain the facts of the dispute as they see them. Then present to each disputant, in as objective a manner as possible, a description of the other party's perception of the problem. Take the opportunity to point out inconsistencies in either party's positions —

they are much more likely to agree to a "clarification of the facts" with you than with the other party. In some cases, this clarification process may be enough to end the dispute.

If not, ask each party to propose potential solutions. Find commonalities among the solutions and see if you can gain agreement on those points by proposing them to each disputant separately. If necessary, suggest solutions of your own. In any case, work step by step to an acceptable compromise.

• **Focus on behavior, not personalities**

Your job as a leader is to make the organization succeed. Your concern in any personal feud, therefore, should not be on trying to bring harmony to a relationship gone sour, but on preventing the conflict from interfering with the functioning of the organization.

As a caring person your natural inclination will be to want everyone on your staff to be on friendly terms at all times. However, unless you are a trained psychologist, you are not likely to be successful in changing people's attitudes toward each other.

But in focusing on behavior patterns you are more likely to have success. Point out to disputants how their behavior is hurting their own performance as well as interfering with the performance of others. Don't allow yourself to get caught up with their personal issues. Focus your attention and theirs on changing their detrimental behavior.

Conflict is as normal a part of the life of a child care center as Legos® and finger jello. By being out front in dealing with conflict as it occurs, a director can create a positive force out of the daily clash of ideas, opinions, and personalities.

Resources

Caplow, T. (1983). *Managing an Organization.* New York: Holt, Rinehart and Winston, 1983.

Quick, T. L. (1977). *Person to Person Managing.* New York: St. Martin's Press.

Training and Supporting Caregivers Who Speak a Language Different From Those in Their Community

by Joan Matsalia and Paula Bowie

"Close your eyes for a minute. Imagine you, or someone you love, is sick. It's serious and you need medical help. You find yourself in the hospital, but no one there speaks the same language as you. You are trying to explain your concern, but see blank stares. Someone hands you paperwork to fill out, but you can't read the words. Think about how you are feeling, and if it involves someone else, how you are trying to comfort them . . . ."

This scenario is a visualization exercise that is one part of a workshop we've designed, and used, around the United States and at the 2003 World Forum on Early Care and Education in Acapulco, México. Our goal has been to engage those in early care and education in a discussion of how to best identify, ensure, and support quality training for those who speak languages other than the dominant language. The above visualization exercise is a simple method to use when seeking to *sensitize* participants to the often overlooked and seldom discussed needs of others in their community.

Why would a couple of white, monolingual women, like us, even be interested in this topic? We feel passionate concerning the right of all children to receive the highest quality caregiving possible. A study of children in family child care and

relative care, done by the Families and Work Institute, indicates that caregivers with appropriate and relevant training provide the most responsive and developmentally appropriate care for young children. Although we are not trying to suggest that all caregivers without formal training lack an understanding of responsive caregiving, we do believe the research indicates that without appropriate training caregivers for many young children are not fully equipped to provide the highest quality care possible. Participants in our workshops have indicated that when designing training for caregivers, the training must be language and geography appropriate, as well as culturally responsive, in order to ensure that caregivers and children are not short-changed.

Throughout the facilitation of these workshops our focus has been to

provide a trusting and comfortable environment along with a format that acknowledges *adult-learner* strategies. One objective has been to create an atmosphere that allows participants to feel safe enough to express the challenges that they confront in their community. (Workshop participants have included trainers, caregivers, college instructors, resource and referral staff, parents, and regulatory administrators.) We discovered that not only in the United States, but also when engaging in dialogue with World Forum delegates from all corners of the world, there is some consensus regarding the challenges many caregivers experience. Furthermore, many of the challenges appear interrelated.

For instance, how do you identify and reach out to those who speak the language and understand the culture of the caregivers you are working with? And how do you ensure that this person's input is an integral part of developing the training in order to convey respect and sensitivity to the caregivers? If this person isn't educated in early care and education, can you access funding for training the trainer, or do you have a mentor program to work with this essential individual? In addition, when language is the only variable, some participants have questioned if the training of the non-dominant caregivers can parallel the same standards as the training the dominant caregivers receive.

We have also come to realize that in some communities the caregivers do not have a written language. Several participants who identified themselves as trainers during our workshops drew attention to a number of cases when trainers are working with caregivers who rely on oral communication, as there is no written language. Still, others noted the lack of written materials available in the language of *comfort*. There is a further paradox when institutions of higher education only offer training in the dominant language. Participants also discussed that the lack of a high school diploma, or access to those records, can be an immediate barrier to college level courses. Some challenges may involve the access to "appropriate trainers."

In situations where same language trainers cannot be located within the community, many participants felt you should begin by determining what kind of on-going anti-bias and sensitivity training is being offered to local trainers. Participants noted concern that without appropriate training the value of others may not be fully realized. As a strategy, one trainer suggested that trainers be given a demonstration exercise whereby they are given an assignment in a language they don't know as a way to *feel* the situation encountered by those who speak another language. Another reminded us it's not just the same language that's a concern, in fact, she explained, "Don't assume that a common language means the same culture." These situations are very real. Without our thoughtful, proactive, collective voice children of the next generation may be negatively impacted. Despite what often felt like overwhelming challenges, workshop

participants were able to uncover strategies.

We are grateful to have acquired suggestions about where to begin this process. When participants began to pool their collective experiences we all learned a great deal. Trainers suggested collaborating with other local programs that have already developed appropriate materials. Others suggested beginning training with a non-threatening needs assessment that helps participants to identify their needs as well as their learning styles. Repeating material in multiple learning styles to ensure understanding has been suggested, as well as addressing specific needs of participants such as transportation to the training site, offering meals, and discovering the best day and time to hold the training.

As participants shared these personal, yet professional, experiences in working with caregivers, we began to develop proactive strategies. A World Forum participant shared her observation that when modeling basic developmentally appropriate practice in the caregiver's own language, she sees an increase in the self-esteem of the caregiver. A participant in a different workshop reminded others to allow caregivers in a community to tell you what they themselves feel they need. In fact, a recurring theme has been to be open to working with people at different levels, by adapting training and materials to meet caregivers where they are. In order to meet caregiver needs, appropriate resources are essential. Uncovering resources was informative because often the resources are people and places, not written documents.

The following is a list of strategy ideas and specific resources gathered during our workshop sessions:

- *Map* all training opportunities (Head Start, college, Resource and Referral, etc.) so as to maximize and not duplicate.

- Cultivate someone who has potential — help potential trainers get what they need — be their mentor.

- Let the people in the community tell *us* what *they* need.

- Get to know the people in the community — "walk a mile in their shoes."

- Provide/develop a *buddy system* for those with like languages and cultures.

- Solicit support from funding sources to provide materials in the home language and the adopted languages.

- Take a stand for the rights of caregivers to receive appropriate training.

- Be open to genuinely seeking out and understanding cultural issues.

- Provide anti-bias and culturally relevant training to trainers.

- Link/network with other programs and communities who have already created appropriate materials.

- Advocate for the development of oral and hands-on training opportunities.

- Genuinely listen to hear the concerns of the caregivers.

- Encourage agencies to hire caregivers from the community.

- Find ways to also offer training to unregulated caregivers.

- Search out local groups such as the school system, faith-based organizations and groups, civic associations, local resource and referral agencies, private trainers and consultants, food sponsors, the Internet, cultural groups/clubs, IRS, Chamber of Commerce, Police Department, court system, colleges, exchange programs, ESL programs, public library, individuals with community connections.

■ Above all else, network at every opportunity locally and in other states.

In closing, we'd like to say that although we've addressed many challenges, and hopefully offered up numerous strategies and resources to help us deal effectively with these challenges, this is merely the tip of the iceberg. Most significant to our struggle is the lack of money to allow for some of these strategies to actually become *initiatives*. Moreover, the universal movement towards standardization and formal education, which is most often only offered in the dominant language of the particular country, continues to undermine truly appropriate training for all caregivers.

We are extremely grateful to the many people who contributed to this article through their honest and open sharing during the workshops held. We facilitated seven workshops between 2001 and 2003 with approximately 110 participants.

Joan Matsalia is the co-president of Boston AEYC, and a Member-at-Large on the National Association for Family Child Care Board of Directors. She operates an accredited family child care program with two full-time assistants. Joan has her Master's Degree in Education and teaches early childhood courses part time. In addition, Joan works part time as the Training Coordinator for Acre Family Day Care, a family child care system located in Lowell, Massachusetts. In this job Joan works primarily with Spanish and South East Asian caregivers developing training programs to best meet their needs. This been a great fit for Joan who has been involved in research related to the training and support available for caregivers who speak languages other than English for the past several years.

Together with Paula Bowie, she has developed a nationally recognized workshop that brings together others in the field to share strategies and lessons learned in the hopes of high quality training for all caregivers, thus increasing the quality of care for all our young children. Joan is married to Frank Matsalia and the proud mother of Shannon, Samantha, and Taylor. Their family home has included Frank's parents since 1999 and Joan's parents since 1994. One thing that has made their family unique is the blending of cultures. Frank is originally from Kenya, East Africa and Joan was born and raised in Massachusetts.

Paula Bowie is the research and training director at the Institute for Family Child Care Systems at Acre Family Day Care in Lowell, Massachusetts. Paula's work at the Institute has included several research projects concerning quality of care and best practices in family child care systems. Paula has raised three daughters with her husband in Massachusetts. They are currently enjoying sharing in the caregiving of their 8-month-old grandson.

Substitutes — We're the Real Thing!

by Bonnie Neugebauer

The life of a substitute is not an easy one — the very word suggests someone who is not the real thing, someone we must put up with for the interim. The word, usually shortened to "sub," even sounds awful — rather short and low.

Yet it would be hard to come up with a person more sought after than a reliable, effective substitute caregiver. Early childhood programs will desperately search — even beg, borrow, or steal — to find a substitute. But on the job, substitutes often feel neglected, even exploited.

As I worked as a substitute teacher in early childhood programs, I discovered that I sometimes felt most valued before I entered the center. An affirmative response to a plea for help resulted in all sorts of joyful, enthusiastic gratitude — I was made to feel important and helpful. After I began my day's work, I often found myself abandoned, saddled with the worst jobs, and floundering to really take care of children with minimal information and support.

To give a sub his or her due, I would like to focus attention on some often forgotten truths about life as a substitute:

A substitute is a real person

This seems like a pretty straight forward point; but if you are not given a bathroom break, then someone has forgotten that you are real. It's awkward to be unsure, fumbling; but there is much that a center can do to enhance the effectiveness and foster the sense of belonging of the substitute.

A substitute has real needs

A substitute needs to understand the context. No one works effectively in a small, isolated space. Without some sense of the big picture, all of us tend to lose our sense of direction — we feel lonely, unsupported, forgotten.

A first time substitute needs a tour of the center. Show her where different age groups meet and how various rooms and spaces are used. Point out the bathroom. Introduce him to other staff, making special note of people he can turn to for specific kinds of help. Help him see how all the pieces of your program fit together. This is also a good time to fill a substitute in on the center philosophy and a few important rules.

Leslie, the director, mails a substitute packet to me, with the appropriate forms for me to fill out. She asks me to arrive 15 minutes early so that I have time to ask questions and read the routine and instructions for individual children before I begin working.

A substitute needs to feel competent in his working environment. Have someone orient the sub as to where supplies and equipment are located. Clearly define procedures for using and returning toys and equipment. Outline expectations for end of the day clean up. Look at the center from the substitute's point of view when labeling mats and storage and designing charts for routines.

A good way to tell if a classroom is efficiently planned and well labeled and organized is to watch a sub at work. How many fumbles to diaper a child? How many false starts in the search for scissors?

A substitute needs to feel the flow. Map out the routine for the day so that the substitute feels on top of things rather than scrambling behind. Children usually have a pretty good sense of the flow, so they can be helpful. However, a substitute who is dependent on the children for basic information feels vulnerable.

In this program there are nappers, half nappers, and no nappers, which I learn the hard way. My assignment is to get about 18 children to sleep. The mats are already positioned, thanks to the departing teacher. As the children come in from outdoors, we sort through pillows and blankets, do the shoe and bathroom routines, read stories, and relax to soothing music. Just as peace is settling over the room, Paul begins to cry, "I'm a half napper. I'm not supposed to come in yet."

A substitute needs to know how to prepare. Before the sub arrives, she should know exactly what to bring.

A group of 25 three and four year olds is having lunch outdoors in the sunshine. It's a beautiful day, and the children are enjoying all the nooks and hidey places in the bushes for small lunch groups. In this program the children bring their own lunches — no one told me to bring one, so I hungrily join the conversation at the picnic table.

Once you have given instructions, don't change the rules.

I am asked to bring an art activity for pre-kindergartners, but find myself in the three year old room. I don't know where any of the supplies are. Jonathan wants to paint, but I can't find any paper. Finally I discover a stash of old letterhead and tape a sheet to the easel.

Several times I arrived at a program at the appointed day and time to the surprise of the director who had forgotten that she had hired me.

A substitute needs to know your expectations. Clearly define your

expectations for how the substitute will function. Make it easy to fit in and feel competent.

The infant room enjoys a ratio of one caregiver for three babies. Kay is in charge with Rose as her assistant. So I am assigned to care for Caitlin, Graham, and Zoe. Special instructions for each baby are posted near the daily chart. Nap times are staggered, so that most of the time I am watching only two babies. All time not spent in routine care is to be spent playing with the babies.

A substitute needs to feel respected. Once you have hired her, support her in doing her job.

*Nap time. I tell the children that I will read them a story, we will listen to a tape, then we will drift off to sleep. After nap time I promise to read another story. I'm just to my favorite part of **Where The Wild Things Are** when Pauline walks by. "That's not how we do it! Play a record for them."*

A substitute needs to be identifiable. Make sure that everyone else knows that the sub is a sub. Knowing this will enable parents and staff to adjust their expectations and respond supportively. No one wants to be put in a position of feeling embarrassed or inadequate.

I am asked to arrive during nap time, so I sit quietly in a room of sleeping children. It's hard to stay awake. I can hear noises overhead as other groups are working away. A teacher comes by to check that all is well. A mother arrives to pick up Gina. I don't know the names of these children! I don't know where Gina is and I can't find her.

Post a notice on the door identifying the substitute — who she is replacing and the hours she will work. Be sure she wears a name tag that clearly identifies her to parents as a substitute — this enables parents to refer to her by name.

A substitute needs to belong. This is one of the trickiest issues to resolve. A substitute is a temporary part of your program so the issues of belonging are different. There is no history, no peer group (in a way), no future.

Somehow you must make the substitute feel that there is a place for him in your program — even if for only a day. Being sensitive to his needs, clear and generous with your introductions, and supportive in your expectations will help you accomplish this goal.

If you are nurturing a long term relationship with a substitute, consider ways to include her in your staff meetings, training sessions, and staff and parent social occasions. The more a substitute feels part of your program, the more committed she will be to continuing her role or becoming a permanent employee.

Part of belonging in an early childhood program is being able to call children by name. Devise a way of helping a substitute learn the children's names quickly. The best idea I've encountered is to put masking tape name tags on all the children before the sub arrives. Include the children who will be on the playground if that is to be part of the day's duties. Children expect immediate name recognition; having to refer to a wall display just doesn't work.

And perhaps most important and most often overlooked, give your substitute time to say goodbye. Often subs just disappear during nap time or into another responsibility. Making sure that substitutes mark their place with children bestows respect on the feelings of both.

A substitute needs to be a substitute. A sub should not be expected to replace a regular teacher in knowledge and ability to perform without time to learn and observe.

Do not ask a sub:

- to diaper a child who is wary of strangers until they have had a chance to get to know each other,

- to take all responsibility for playground duty unless that is the job you have outlined beforehand,

- to take the children outside the center unless accompanied by regular staff,

- to administer medications,

- to work all day without a break,

- to perform all the onerous tasks — unless you never want to see him again,

- to know policies and procedures if you have not given her the opportunity to learn them, or

- to instantly take the place of a regular staff member in knowledge and ability to perform.

A substitute has hidden potential

Just like everyone else, a substitute will need to talk about her experiences in your program. It's been a stressful day and whether it went well or not, your substitute will be eager to share her adventures. Whom she chooses to talk to and what she chooses to say is up to her but not totally out of your control.

Think of a substitute as a marketing tool. Whether you like it or not, your substitute is going to be doing some word of mouth marketing for your program. Armed with the information he has gathered — facts, impressions, experiences — he will be talking about you. Make sure that your substitute feels part of your program so that he feels invested and speaks from that perspective. If you

give a sub the opportunity to share his experiences and insights with you, he leaves your center feeling valued and will be more likely to put the best light on things.

Think of a substitute as a short term, inexpensive consultant. During her day in your program, the sub will have gathered all sorts of impressions. Because her perspective is different, she will see different things. Some of her observations will be valuable and some will be irritat-

ing. But all of her observations will give you information about your program.

Anika's parents arrive during their lunch hour to be with their six month old. She is sitting in an infant seat, playing with the mobile overhead. Her parents crouch down beside her and talk to her. They play with her fingers, but they do not pick her up. Why?

You might even offer to pay a substitute for an additional half hour of

---

Prepare a Substitute Information Packet

If possible, mail this packet to the substitute so that he can come prepared. Include the following information:

Expectations —
Hours and days to be worked
Pay rate and how payment will be made
What to do upon arrival — whom to report to, where to stow personal items
Breaks — when, where, how
Age group of children

Basic rules —
Smoking
Telephone privileges (include staff phone number if applicable, when phone can be used, any special dialing procedures, whether incoming calls can be accepted and where messages will be posted)
Food (any special foods that may or may not be eaten) also times when it's acceptable to eat

Guidelines —
Discipline — time out/cool off, etc.
Drop off and pick up procedures
Health issues, list of children with special health considerations — food allergies, medications (who and what to administer)
Curriculum — which activities are fixed and which are open to choice

Responsibilities —
Daily routine
Any activities or materials that the substitute should bring/prepare
Clean up — how to know when work is done

Directions —
How to get to the center by car or bus
Which door to enter
Where to park

time to ensure that she will fill out a questionnaire about her day. Or, if time is possible, pay a substitute for a few minutes of direct feedback in conversation with you.

Of course, the substitute carries her own baggage, so you must keep this in mind. Some comments will point to bias, inexperience, or attitude — you can put these into perspective and still find the insights and truths in this one person's feedback.

Think of a substitute as a resource. If you know of special interests and talents, encourage the substitute to share them in the classroom. She might be a gardener, a storyteller, a carpenter, or a musician. This is a wonderful opportunity to bring new experiences to the children; and it gives the sub a special way to become part of things.

A substitute usually has knowledge about other programs in the community. Ask her how other centers solve particular problems and accomplish specific activities. Encourage her to share her valuable expertise.

A substitute responds to love

If you love your substitute, make it as easy as possible for her to be effective. Prepare a substitute information handbook (see box), orient her on site, give her support on the job, and let her know that her good work just might have saved your day. A good substitute is indeed the real thing — a necessary and valuable component of a quality early care and education program.

Countering Center Gossip

by Margaret Leitch Copeland and Holly Elissa Bruno

When asked about their greatest management challenges, a group of Vermont directors mentioned gossip as eroding professionalism in their centers. Two factors contributed to the directors' concerns: 1) during the staffing shortage, new hires are often young, inexperienced, and under-educated, and 2) in small, rural towns, employees know the families enrolled in the program, which creates home and center boundary questions.

Why do staff gossip?

Then when asked *why* staff gossip, the directors were also very clear in saying:

1) Staff members have a need to talk with other adults, and many love to talk

2) Other than common employment, staff members may have little in common with each other so they talk about parents, children, other staff, and the director's decisions

3) People are trying to fit in

4) Passing on information increases a sense of self-worth

5) Staff members have strong feelings of frustration and are looking for a way to release their anger

6) People are looking for support

Gossip is a form of *power*. Gossipers have negative power to influence opinion, to be part of an inner circle, to feel *one up* or *in the know*, to isolate another person who is seen as a threat or to undermine constructive change. One wise director commented that no staff member thinks that the comments he makes or the information he passes along is gossip; that, by definition, gossip is what other people do! Ironically, he also thought that all staff would agree that others need to be stopped from gossiping.

What is the director to do?

The first questions to ask are:

1) Is the center mission clear? Is it a mantra for staff?

2) What is the center policy about gossip? Is there one? Does everybody know it? Are there consequences?

3) Does the director herself inadvertently engage in gossip?

Without a living mission or vision statement, the goal of the center is not clear to staff. Tee shirts, plaques, note cards, and brochures with the mission displayed help get the mission out of the file cabinet and into the life of the center. If staff cannot recite the mission of the center, there is little likelihood they will live it.

What guidance does a director have for creating an anti-gossip policy?

Fortunately, the NAEYC *Code of Ethical Conduct* (1998) provides critical guidance in creating a center policy about gossip:

"Ethical responsibilities to families:

Ideals: I-2.1 To develop relationships of mutual trust with the families we serve . . .

Principles: P-2.9 We shall maintain confidentiality and shall respect the family's right to privacy, refraining from disclosure of confidential information and intrusion into family life."

"Ethical responsibilities to colleagues:

Ideals: I-3A.1 To establish and maintain relationships of respect, trust, and cooperation with co-workers . . .

Principles: P-3A.1 When we have a concern about the professional behavior of a co-worker, we shall first let the person know of our concern, in a way that shows respect for personal dignity and for the diversity to be found among staff members, and then attempt to resolve the matter collegially . . .

Ideals: I-3C.2 To create a climate of trust and candor that will enable staff to speak and act in the best interests of children, families, and the field of early care and education . . .

Principles: P-3C.2 We shall provide staff members with safe and supportive working conditions that permit them to carry out their responsibilities, timely and non-threatening evaluation procedures, written grievance procedures, constructive feedback, and opportunities for continuing professional development and advancement."

The aforementioned directors suggested a policy that would include a definition of gossip and the consequences of gossiping, both to the injured party and to the employee. It would also include a statement that staff is expected to remind colleagues and parents about the confidentiality policy. Depending on the center, the policy may be developed by the board of directors, the director, or in concert with the staff and parents. It should be included in the staff handbook and posted in the staff lounge. The purpose of the policy is to create a culture of safety, encouragement and respect that is consistent with the *Code*.

It is important for staff to understand the purpose of the policy and to

buy into upholding it. Sometimes it is not obvious to staff what is considered gossip or confidential information and what is simply common knowledge and shared information.

The Vermont directors suggested this activity for a staff meeting to clarify the difference between gossip or negative talk and common knowledge or shared information:

**Confidential or
Not Confidential,
That is Part of the Question!**
(The Other Part is the Intent!)

1) The director listens for examples of inappropriate comments and carefully camouflages them to depersonalize the content. Then she makes up some outrageous examples, or perhaps uses real ones from her past. She writes enough vignettes on note cards so that each staff member can have one. Examples might be:
   a) At circle time, Charlie tells about his mother's boyfriend hitting her last night
   b) The director has a new Monica Lewinski crocheted pocketbook
   c) Tiffany's father had on his jogging suit this morning and didn't look like he was going to work
   d) The board of directors is voting tonight on our raises for next year
   e) Misty has a cigarette burn on her hand
   f) The new staff member always wears long sleeves, even in summer
   g) Tony's aunt who has a child in another classroom wants to know how he's doing
   h) The teaching teams are going to be different next year; Cheryl is going to get demoted
   i) Tyrone got expelled from another center before he came here
   j) Charnetta's mother couldn't pay her child care bill this month

   k) The Paperback Kiddie Book Klub money is missing and Juanita has new earrings
2) At the staff meeting, a hat is passed and everyone takes a card. The director creates small groups, making sure to divide up established gossip partners. The groups are then charged with deciding:
   a) Is this confidential information?
   b) Is it accurate? Or gossip? Or rumor?
   c) With whom should it be discussed? Should it be documented?
   d) What is the intent of sharing this information? Helpful or harmful?
   e) If you were the other person, would you want it discussed?
   f) Are there safety issues (abuse, neglect, etc.) to be considered?
   g) Is time essential or can you think about it first?
   h) How would you recommend someone deal with this?
   i) How does the *Code of Ethical Conduct* apply?
3) Finally, groups report to each other.
4) The director then makes it clear what the policy is and what the consequences will be for violating it, as well as the unintended consequences for the innocent families and staff being discussed.

Knowing that adults do not always change their behavior just because there is a policy created and that people need some practice when a new behavior is expected, the director plans some role-plays for the next staff meeting. Again, he has created scenarios based on veiled local examples and typical dilemmas faced in early care and education. Staff is divided into dyads chosen in advance by the director: one person who does not have clear boundaries about gossip and one who does. There should be enough role-plays so that each participant gets to play the person who is trying to uphold the confidentiality policy and then to switch and play the opposite role.

The director makes a chart of phrases that are appropriate when a staff member is asked an inappropriate question: Didn't I see Brenda (teacher) at the Stark Brewery on Friday? Is Sally pregnant or is she just gaining weight? How could he afford that car? Is Kenny still biting? Do you think she had artificial insemination? The director circulates, listening for the phrases and reinforcing appropriate responses. The second meeting ends with an ultimatum clarifying the policy, the expected behaviors, and the warnings and terminations that may result if the expectations are not met.

One director reports that she writes up incidents and includes them in annual evaluations with examples of how gossip has gotten out of hand. She finds that staff who are in their first real jobs, dealing with many personalities, need explicit guidance. Finally, the director must assiduously avoid any temptation to listen to the gossip that she abhors. She must articulate the mission, confront gossip and negativity immediately and promote peer responsibility to do the same. In this era of shortages in staffing, some directors report that they are loath to let any staff go and thus feel powerless to take action. Others report that the gossiper is a good worker otherwise and that drawing a line in the sand may result in the termination of a valued teacher. But other staff members are demoralized by the culture of gossip and are watching to see the director's response to negativity and overt breaches of confidentiality.

What about parents? How can the director impact their conversations with staff?

Helping parents understand the policy may require modifications of the activities used with staff. It is important to put the confidentiality policy in the parent handbook and to explain it at parent meetings. Instead of role plays, skits done by the staff may help parents see how they benefit from confidentiality and how some of their questions about who bites or has head lice may seem innocuous at first, but inappropriate on second look. One seasoned director notes that first-time parents simply haven't thought about the confidentiality they would like to be afforded, and thus ask such questions quite spontaneously.

One center distributes the *Code of Ethical Conduct* to parents with a letter explaining it. Their parent handbook gives examples of how staff must adhere to the *Code*. At first, when staff referred to the *Code*, parents were surprised to hear that their questions were considered inappropriate; but then when they thought about reversing roles, they would not have wanted their children's behavior commented upon by staff to another parent.

How can the director get staff to confront each other when they hear gossip?

Staff need training on how to confront each other on gossip without falling prey to the *shame-blame game,* which only leads to defensiveness. Four key principles make for effective peer-to-peer confrontations:

1) Each person gets equal time to state the problem without being interrupted (a timer may help).
2) Active listening is required; paraphrasing what she has heard is allowable.
3) Phrases like "You should . . . " or "You shouldn't . . . " are not appropriate, but phrases from the training are: "Is this confidential?" "Why do I need to know this?" "If you were . . . would you want this discussed?"

4) Referring to the center's mission or the *Code of Ethical Conduct* keeps the discussion on a higher, depersonalized level.

The director can help by creating spaces where adults can sit and talk with each other with the door closed. She can also provide mediation when two staff members are not getting along. But primarily, when trained in appropriate techniques, staff can provide coaching on peer confrontation for each other. The coach guides each person to state her version of the problem, to say what she needs, to brainstorm possible solutions without criticism, and to agree on common ground.

Because this process is a radical change from the indirectness of gossip and negativity, resistance is likely initially, but it becomes futile when the center culture changes to empower staff to confront ethical conflicts among their peers.

In *The Visionary Director* (1998), Carter and Curtis include a Conflict Resolution Agreement (p. 245), which may be helpful to directors trying to help staff take responsibility for confronting one another on gossip.

But what will staff talk about?

In the absence of gossip, just how much can people talk about the weather? The reasons why people gossip have not changed. The director may find that he needs to influence the conversation in small ways; talking about changing the environment or enriching the curriculum, asking if teachers have read the latest article in *Exchange* or suggesting an upcoming workshop may need to be a very conscious effort to change the center conversational culture. Discussing plans for upcoming center events and what roles individual staff members will play can help people feel part of the team.

Giving staff enough ventilation time in supervision sessions can help with the feeling of frustration that early childhood educators feel when they are not well compensated for difficult and meaningful work. One director suggests that using some staff meeting time for expressions of frustration keep staff from exploding at parents and children.

Increasing staff appreciation strategies can help with feelings of self-worth and daily conversation with every staff member will create a sense of support from the director.

One director of a program with multiple sites puts out a daily newsletter with accurate information, including birthdays, employment anniversaries, substitutes working that day. She has found that by creating appropriate news items she is able to counter trivial gossip and rumor.

Another director takes every staff member individually out to lunch in February. After an initial awkwardness, she learns their dreams and concerns, and they enjoy having her undivided attention. She is able to tailor her questions to their professional developmental levels and to insert the kind of conversation she would like to hear in the center.

"The gossip problem is never totally gone," cautions another director. "We need to keep talking and asking how we are doing. If we don't, gossip keeps creeping into the center."

Most of all, the director must model loyalty to the center mission, use the phrases, and keep asking the questions from the first exercise: What is the intent of telling that? Who needs to know? Is this helpful information? How does this advance the mission of the center? One director is careful to check with parents: "Is this something you want shared with other staff?" A gossip-free center culture supports everyone in the center community and eventually helps them focus on the mission and the work to be done on behalf of children and families.

References

Carter, M., & Curtis, D. (1998). *The visionary director: A handbook for dreaming, organizing and improvising in your center.* St. Paul, MN : Redleaf Press.

Chittendon County (Vermont) Directors Association (1999). Workshop conversations and charts.

Code of ethical conduct and statement of commitment; Guidelines for responsible behavior in early childhood education. (1998). Washington, DC: National Association for the Education of Young Children.

Special thanks to the Cittendon County (Vermont) Directors Association for many ideas used in this article.

Margaret Leitch Copeland, Ed.D., is the Administrator of the Child Development Bureau at the New Hampshire Department of Health and Human Services.

Holly Elissa Bruno, J.D., heads Bruno Duraturo Consulting in Concord, Massachusetts. Both teach graduate seminars around the country for the Centers for Career Development in Early Care and Education at Wheelock College.

Overcoming the Fear of Firing

Ideas from 30 Directors

"It was obvious that this teacher could not relate well to kids. But I could not bring myself to fire her . . . and while I wavered, things only got worse for everyone in her classroom."

Having to fire someone is probably the most difficult action a director may have to take. It is an action for which directors can find endless excuses to avoid, as did the director quoted above. But it is an action which in certain cases must be taken.

To discover how directors can overcome their fear of firing and to learn what precautions to take and what mistakes to avoid in the firing process, *Exchange* surveyed 30 early childhood directors who had fired an employee. The suggestions that follow are based on their experiences and recommendations.

When is firing appropriate?

People who go into a social service such as early care and education typically care very much about individuals. However, directors are also responsible for caring for the organization as a whole and for the families it serves. When the needs of an individual staff member come into serious conflict with the needs of the

group, the director must place higher priority on the welfare of the group.

The directors identified four areas where the performance of individual staff members most frequently detracts from the performance of the organization to the extent that firing may be necessary. The four areas, listed in order of frequency of occurrence are:

1. Poor work habits — Chronic lateness and absenteeism; shirking of job responsibilities; sloppy, careless work. One director reported firing a teacher who "sat most of the time and shouted across the room instead of going to talk to a child. I found her sleeping in the nap room rather than watching the nappers."

2. Sub-par job performance — Inability to satisfactorily perform job responsibilities; inability to develop necessary skills. Specific problems cited include "lack of behavior management skills," "inability to supervise assistant teachers," "lack of empathy and patience with

children," and "inability to plan appropriate activities."

3. Unacceptable behavior — Behavior which is detrimental to children, staff, or the organization. Typically these behaviors relate to inappropriate disciplining of children such as "striking a child," "verbally abusing children," "locking a child in the bathroom," or "attacking children's self-images." Some directors also cited situations where staff members disrupted the organization by "refusing to cooperate with other teachers," or by "inciting disharmony and negativism among the teachers."

4. Policy violations — Unwillingness to conform to center policies and philosophies. A wide range of incidents were cited here including "stealing center property," "violating the confidentiality of parent conversations," "refusal to adapt to the curriculum approach of the school," and "coming to work intoxicated."

Potential problems

The process of firing an employee is never a pleasant one. During the period when the director is weighing the decision and then waiting to announce it, he or she typically experiences considerable anxiety. The conference at which the employee is notified of the decision is often loaded with tension and tears or anger and ill-will. Then, if the employee reacts poorly to the action, the director may experience guilt.

Occasionally, more serious problems occur. When an employee perceives that she is being fired unjustly, she may seek to rally support among the other teachers and parents. This can lead to a period of internal conflict and leave a residue of hard feelings.

When there is a level of authority above the person who did the firing, such as an owner, a board of directors, a regional director, or a sponsoring agency, the terminated employee occasionally will appeal the decision. This appeal may proceed through normal channels such as a grievance procedure, or it may take a more personal direction. In one instance, an employee sent letters to every board member, claiming foul play by the director and demanding immediate reinstatement. In another instance, the spouse of a terminated employee appeared at the door of the center's owner threatening a law suit.

A confrontation may also occur if the terminated employee is denied unemployment benefits and appeal this ruling. In many states an employee who is fired may have a claim for unemployment benefits judged to be "unapprovable" if he was fired for gross misconduct or for misdeeds directed against the employer. The information for making this decision comes from the former employer. If the former employee appeals a decision, the director may then be required to attend a hearing. One director who attended such a hearing found it very unpleasant "to be discussing the employee's poor work record in front of her, her husband, and the hearing officer."

In some cases the repercussions are even more unpleasant. Several directors reported receiving angry or obscene phone calls at home from the terminated worker for weeks after the firing. One was physically threatened. In another case the former employee dedicated herself to spreading vicious rumors about the center and the director in the community.

Although such negative outcomes do occur when the firing process misfires, they need not be the inevitable consequence. Three-fourths of the directors interviewed indicated that the positive results of firing an unsatisfactory employee far outweighed the negative ones. In most cases the morale of the staff eventually, if not immediately, improved.

Laying the groundwork

The directors surveyed had many recommendations for avoiding the negative consequences of the firing process. Many of these had to do with laying the groundwork, with actions that should be taken even before the final decision to fire is made.

• **Establish Guidelines.** All personnel working in a center should know, from the day they join the center, what actions or behaviors on their part can result in their being fired. These policies should be in writing, and they should be given to all staff members or posted in a conspicuous place. Staff members have a right to know these ground rules. Once they know them, their responsibility to abide by them should not be subject to questions at the termination.

Most centers surveyed have two categories of offenses in their policies. One category is for flagrant actions which are cause for immedi-

ate termination. Cited as examples of such offenses were striking a child, leaving children unattended, inflicting harsh punishments, gross negligence, and being intoxicated on the job.

• **Establish a Grievance Procedure.** If at all possible employees should have some means of appealing major personnel actions such as a firing. This may consist of a hearing before an owner, an executive director, a personnel committee, or a special grievance panel. Having such a procedure established in advance gives an aggrieved employee a clear recourse and helps prevent unnecessary parties from becoming involved in the dispute.

• **Review Performance Periodically.** Once employees' work habits or performance have degenerated to the point where a termination is warranted, it may no longer be possible for them to radically alter their behavior. If the director is concerned with the welfare of individual employees and wishes to help them avoid termination, she should perform periodic performance reviews for all employees. Poor habits and substandard performance should be brought to the employee's attention before it gets out of hand. In these reviews the director or supervisor should help the employee set goals for improvement as well as offer whatever support the center can muster. Progress toward meeting these goals should then be closely monitored.

• **Give Adequate Warning.** Nearly every director emphasized that there should be "no surprises." As soon as it becomes apparent to the director that an employee may need to be fired, that employee should be warned that such an action is being considered. This warning should be given in a private conference between the director and the employee. The directors recommend that in this conference the employee should be told:

1) the specific center policies the employee is violating or failing to adhere to;

2) objective examples or anecdotes which demonstrate this claim;

3) the specific changes required of the employee to avoid being fired;

4) how the employee's effort to make these changes will be monitored; and

5) the deadline for the final evaluation.

Some centers have a formal two or three step notification process. In one center the director is required to give a preliminary verbal warning, an initial written warning, and a final written warning before issuing a notification of termination. However, if a center has an effective performance review process, the early warnings needed to give the employee a fair opportunity to improve should be coming up in the periodic reviews.

Since warning conferences can become quite emotional, key messages sometimes fail to get communicated. Sometimes directors try too hard to cushion the blow by sugarcoating the warning. In one instance a director went to such lengths emphasizing the employee's strong points in addition to the problem areas that the employee left the meeting unaware that she was close to being fired. A second message often delivered unclearly is what specific steps the employee needs to take to meet the director's expectations. To avoid miscommunication, one

director suggested having the employee state his interpretation of the director's message to be sure he has an accurate understanding of it.

- **Keep Written Records.** As one director urged — "Document! Document! Document!" Keep a record of periodic performance reviews, incidents of unsatisfactory performance, conferences where warnings are administered or terminations are announced. Some directors also issue warnings and terminations in writing as well as verbally. Other directors, dealing with a particularly unstable or vindictive employee, request that the employee sign a written summary of a warning or termination conference to attest to the fact that the summary is accurate (not that they necessarily agree with it).

Documentation such as this serves two purposes. First, it ensures that the director's message is conveyed. All people's memories of conversations are distorted by emotions and expectations. So it is quite likely that an employee coming out of an emotional warning conference will have a faulty memory of the specifics, unless the memory is aided by a written summary.

Second, documentation provides insurance for post-termination confrontations. If the employee challenges a firing, either before an owner, a board, or an unemployment claims officer, claiming that adequate warning was not given or that the reasons are groundless, a written record of the entire process should provide sufficient evidence to counter these claims.

- **Keep Employees Informed.** Another means of avoiding potential confrontation is for the director to keep her employer up-to-date on the situation. For a director who is also the owner of the business, of

course, there is no one else to turn to. However, if the director answers to a board, an owner, an executive director, a regional director, or a sponsoring agency, the appropriate party should be consulted as soon as the possibility of a termination arises. The privacy of the employee must be respected, so prior consultations should be made in confidence. One director kept the board's chairperson advised, rather than discussing the situation with the full board. When the terminated employee appealed to the board, the chairperson was able to verify the director's account of the process.

Completing the process

Once the termination process is set in motion, a clear conclusion is necessary. The following are the directors' recommendations on minimizing the negative effects of the final act on the employee, the director, and the organization.

- **Make the Decision Objectively.** It is, of course, impossible to remove all emotion from a termination decision. How you feel about the person, how the decision will affect the individual and his family, and how it will affect the staff all will influence the decision consciously or unconsciously. The director should not try to deny these emotions but should try to keep them in perspective so that they will not cause a bad decision to be made.

One way to keep issues in perspective is to avoid making a termination decision while under stress or in a crisis. When a teacher arrives 30 minutes late thereby causing the director to miss a meeting, the director may in anger be tempted to fire the teacher on the spot. Weighing the incident later in a calmer mood, the director may realize that this was one of the few times the teacher had ever been late and that to fire her would be seriously overreacting.

Another technique for maintaining perspective is to list all the specific pieces of evidence where the employee is in fact violating center policies or failing to perform her work responsibilities. Then assess whether this list is serious enough to justify termination.

If the evidence warrants termination, the director should then weigh the other negative consequences of the termination — i.e., the impact on the individual, his family, the center, the children, the parents — to determine if the firing can be handled in such a way as to ameliorate these consequences. For example — could the employee be slotted into a less demanding job in the organization? Could the terms of the firing be stated in such a way that the employee can receive unemployment? Could the employee be given an opportunity to save face by resigning first?

Another consideration at this point is setting the employee's last work day. In general it is in everyone's best interest for the employee to leave immediately. Once the employee is fired she may find it embarrassing to continue working at the center. In other cases an embittered person may make life miserable for the staff or the director by stirring up trouble in the final days. In such circumstances it may be best to pay the employee severance pay for one or two weeks rather than keeping her

on the job. In other cases where feelings are less damaged, it may be helpful to allow the employee to stay on until she can find another job.

• **Notifying the Employee Directly.** Once the termination decision has been made, the employee should be told as soon as possible in a private conference. Preferably, this should occur at the end of the day to protect the employee from confronting the other staff members when leaving. Without prolonging the agony by chit-chatting about the weather, the director should tell the employee of the decision in clear and simple terms. If this meeting has been properly prepared for, the decision should not be unexpected. Any sugarcoating or beating around the bush will only confuse the issue.

The director should state the specific reasons for the termination. There may be other unsatisfactory aspects of the employee's performance, such as sloppy dress, bad attitude, or poor relations with staff or parents; but if these are not the reasons for which the employee is being fired, they should not be mentioned in this conference.

The director should also be prepared to answer all the employee's contractual questions, such as what the appeal process is, when the last day will be, whether severance pay and unused vacation time will be granted, and whether the director will write a job recommendation for the employee in the future. All

important points should, of course, be included in a termination letter given to the employee during the conference.

In certain circumstances the director may be inclined to offer the employee help in applying for benefits or in finding a new job. This fact should be stated. But the director should not press to offer help unless the employee specifically asks for it.

• **Announce the Action Honestly.** The other employees, and in some cases the parents, will have an extreme interest in the action. If they are not informed, eventually the rumor mill will begin generating distorted versions of what happened. Such rumors can have a negative impact on staff morale and staff-director relations. Therefore, the staff and parents should be informed about the termination as soon as possible and as honestly as possible without violating the former employee's privacy by revealing details.

If the employee was popular among the staff and parents, they may find fault with the decision. But the director should not attempt to regain their approval by revealing confidential information or by reversing the decision. More likely than not, however, staff members will be more relieved than angered by the decision. Twenty-eight of the thirty directors reported that staff members reacted positively to termination decisions.

Healing Staff After a Termination

by Diana S. Khanagov

"As a new director the biggest mistake I made was under-estimating the impact of a termination on the rest of the staff," *says Pam Scott, a director of a human resources department for Integris. Whether it is a teacher who shirks responsibilities or reliable teachers dismissed because of downsizing, termination affects everyone.*

A director's response to situations leading to termination helps the healing process, The key is damage control. Establish a plan for corrective action before you need it. The corrective action plan serves three purposes: it gives employees opportunities to change; it demonstrates that the director can be trusted to handle matters fairly; and, as the process continues, it prepares other staff members for the termination of their teammate.

The physical, emotional, and mental well-being of children cannot be compromised; therefore, some situations and behaviors must result in immediate termination. These should be written in the center's policy handbook. But what about the caregiver having difficulty keeping up with requirements or adapting to the center's improvements for quality care?

Larry Harrell, co-director and owner of Southwest Child Development Center in Oklahoma City, says: "Endangering or belittling a child means immediate termination. My wife, Jana, and I ask ourselves, 'Is this a person who will represent this center in a positive manner? Is this a one-time incident? Does this person need some training on a particular issue?' An important aspect for us is 'What is this person doing for children?' There are all kinds of avenues. We could cut back on hours, change their hours — give them a new routine. It's really hard to give up on a good staff person. If you've had them four or five years, you just don't want to walk in and fire them. Before I hired them, I had to believe in them."

Begin with a method for evaluation. Employees must know what is inadequate about their job performance before they can choose what is best for them, whether it be a change in their job performance or a change in employment. Shop around for evaluation ideas. Ask other directors how they evaluate staff. Check resources such as the Internet and the library for books about management styles. Don't overlook books written for businesses other than early care and education. Borrow features from corporate job evaluations, then add features specific only to the field of early care and education. Whatever form you choose, the evaluation is a tool that tells staff how you perceive the quality of their work.

How far will you go to help an employee? Some directors help the teacher find extra training, troubleshoot problems, and create a plan of action. When opportunities for change have been exhausted, it's time to say good-bye. Keeping a teacher who performs poorly lowers morale and encourages resentment from teammates. Their continued employment sends the wrong message to staff who go over and above the standards you have set for the center.

According to staff members, one damaging result of dismissal is the corrosion of trust, the most essential element between employee and employer. Trust is compromised when staff members witness a director fire someone on a whim, reacting on impulse to a situation. One director created an unproductive work environment by threatening, "If you blink wrong, I can fire you." Staff members reported difficulty concentrating on work for fear of the rug being yanked out from under them. "If the director is trusted, then it's a ripple in everyday life. If the director is not the leader and is mistrusted, then a termination can turn into a mob scene. It takes about two years for the group to become cohesive again."

Staff members prefer to hear about the dismissal from the director instead of hearing it through the grapevine. "Don't act as if nothing happened. When our director was fired, there was no announcement. There wasn't any thought given to the feelings of the staff."

"Sometimes you hear it from the grapevine first, but the director should still tell the staff as soon as possible. Don't wait for the regular staff meeting."

How a director tells the staff is a matter of personal style. Strive for a professional, sincere explanation without gritty details and hints of sarcasm. Pam Scott says: "I would say, 'This was a business decision. We are here to care for children. We have standards that we can no longer compromise. This person decided that she could not meet those standards. I want to assure you that I got all of the information and facts before making this decision. I treated this person fairly.' The aftermath depends on how well the person was liked. A great person can do a bad job." Sometimes termination means losing someone who you value personally. "It's fine to acknowledge the person's good points, but it is still a business decision."

"Even if you don't give details, they will talk about it. Women have to talk about it to process it. They are more likely than men to have deeper friendships with colleagues." Negative remarks about the employee's lack of work ethics interfere with healing. In the weeks following a termination, your team may find themselves picking up the ex-employee's unfinished business or discovering more inadequacies in the person's work habits. Negative comments prolong "getting back to normal" to a healthful, caring, productive environment. Constant energy spent on negative issues can result in low morale — which is even harder to overcome than the loss of a

---

Is This Normal?

Take a look at how some directors feel after the loss of a staff member.

Susan Bates, Director; University of Oklahoma Children's World; Norman, Oklahoma:

"It depends on the circumstances. I think you're always sad. Sometimes you know it's just not a good fit. In order for you to feel fair about it afterwards, you have to let them know it was coming. It helps to know that you addressed the issues and gave them an opportunity to change. We tell them in at least three different ways. It gives them a chance to resign on their own.

"It's also a big disappointment. You hired them because you like them. You checked their references and invested time and energy because you thought it was going to work."

Priscilla Alley, Director; New Horizons West; Edmond, Oklahoma:

"I'm used to it. I still don't like to do it, but it's part of the job and it has to be done. It has to be done for the good of the center and the rest of the staff."

Priscilla absolutely agrees that a low performer lowers overall morale. "It makes everyone's job harder. The rest of the staff end up getting upset with the director and asking, 'Why don't you do something?' If we don't do anything, they see it as our weakness."

Paula Hulstine, Director; New Horizons; Edmond, Oklahoma:

"It depends on why I terminate them. If it's during their probation period, then I haven't gotten to know them well. If it's not working out for them in the probation period, they are usually frustrated themselves. They are relieved to know they can go on to something else. When it's someone who has worked for me for a while, I feel very sad. I feel sad for them, sad for me, and sad for the children. Change is hard for the children too.

"Another feeling that people may not expect is feeling like a failure. You feel like a failure if you worked with the person to get past the problem and nothing helped."

teammate. Instead, direct your staff's focus on working together efficiently to repair damages.

Some teachers may be relieved if the termination process created tension in the workplace or if they carried the employee's workload over a long period. No matter how lazy or adversarial the ex-employee, count on at least one staff member who enjoyed her friendship, understood her problems, and feels sorry for her plight. Some staff may struggle with issues of loyalty. However the lines of relationships cross, expect your staff to grieve over the loss. Stages of grief may include shock, anger, and sadness.

Two weeks after an employee was immediately dismissed, a remaining staff member said, "I think we're just now getting over the shock, now we're getting angry." Other staff members reported signs of depression, 'I don't feel like doing anything,' and feeling nauseous when the new employee showed up to fill the position. "It's a dilemma because you don't want to blame the new person."

Pam Scott says: "Some staff even experience 'survivor's guilt,' especially if they contributed in any way to the person's job loss. Guilt keeps on giving. Spend time one on one. Reassure everyone that they have a responsibility not just to the person fired but to themselves and to the business. It's an ongoing process. Check back frequently asking, 'What other questions do you have?' and 'How are you feeling?'"

A decline in morale was commonly noted by early childhood staff. "Termination definitely affects morale. You begin to wonder — if it happened to her, it could happen to me." What's a sign of low morale? Several teachers reported a lack of interest in work that gradually diminished with time. Signs of lingering low morale are increased sick leave, arriving late for work, and a lack of interest in the workplace traditions, such as celebrating achievements, birthdays, and holidays. One agency that supports early care and education programs chose not to celebrate the holidays with their traditional office party for the first time in 25 years — no tinsel, no lights, not even holiday music. Not one employee attended the holiday party of another agency that lays off a large number of employees every December. The sarcasm behind the "get-over-it" attitude widens the gap between director and staff. Eventually it undermines morale.

Low morale is like stepping on a piece of gum. It's most likely to happen when you're not paying attention. And if you're really oblivious to gum on your shoe, it affects every place you walk! The longer low morale continues, the more difficult it is to clean up. Long-term low morale leads to an overall careless attitude that, without proper attention, becomes the norm. New staff detect it without any explanation from other staff. It is a serious handicap for a teamleader.

Expect some staff members to continue a personal relationship with the ex-employee. A divisive misconception is that staff must choose sides, their ex-teammate or their director. Sometimes it's an unspoken request or a verbal threat. One director told staff, "You will reap the consequence if you continue to talk to this person."

Just as negative remarks about the ex-employee affect the work environment, so a continued friendship focused on contempt for the director or the workplace breeds bad attitudes. Negativity, on either side of the coin, feeds tension that ultimately prevents a caring environment for children.

Coach your staff to recognize harmful attitudes that compromise the goal of the team — to provide a loving, caring atmosphere where children can develop naturally. Encourage and engage in conversations and actions that build a stronger team. Begin by acknowledging what it means to lose a teammate. "The biggest mistake I made was underestimating the impact a termination has on the rest of the staff."

*Diana S. Khanagov is a freelance writer who lives in Midwest City, Oklahoma. She is a contributing author of **The Parents' & Teachers' Guide to Helping Young Children Learn: Creative Ideas From 35 Respected Experts**.*

Additional Staffing Resources
from *Exchange*

Books:

The Art of Leadership: Managing Early Childhood Organizations
250 Management Success Stories
Does Your Team Work?
The Anti-Ordinary Thinkbook
Places for Childhoods

Exchange Articles on CD Collections:

Supervising Staff
Avoiding Burnout
Staff Training
Taking Stock — Evaluation Tools for Program, Teacher, and Director

Out of the Box Training Kits in the following categories:

Health and Safety
Curriculum Development and Implementation
Environments
Family Partnerships
Professionalism
Early Care and Education
Infants and Toddlers
Observation, Assessment, and Documentation
Positive Discipline

To learn more about and to order these and other Exchange resources, go to
www.ChildCareExchange.com.